THE ARCH LECTURES

THE ARCH LECTURES

BY CLAUDE BRAGDON

Eighteen discourses on a great variety of
subjects delivered in New York,
during the winter of 1940

Essay Index in Reprint

Core Collection Books, inc.
GREAT NECK, NEW YORK

First Published 1942
Reprinted 1978

Library of Congress — Catalog Card No. 77-092505

International Standard Book Number
0-8486-3000-9

PRINTED IN THE UNITED STATES OF AMERICA

Portrait of the Author

INTRODUCTION

THIS IS TO INFORM THE READER HOW THESE LECTURES came to be given. It all began with a chance question asked me by Carman Barnes: Had I any ideas about the teaching of young people the things necessary for them to learn to save their lives from shipwreck. She had been expelled from a fashionable girls' school at the age of sixteen for telling the truth about it in a book, *Schoolgirl*, which sold thirty-five thousand copies, was made into a play and into a movie. Miss Barnes went on writing books about the revolt of the younger generation, increasingly overcome, with all her knowingness, with a sense of her essential ignorance. Filled with imaginings of the kind of a school she would herself like to go to, and a growing determination to "do something about it," she sought everywhere for the answer to her question.

As it happened, I had myself been a teacher in a fashionable girls' school for a short time, and this experience had given me ideas and opinions which I proceeded to unfold. When I had finished, Miss Barnes asked me if I would be willing to repeat what I had just told her to a group of her friends whom she hoped to interest. This resulted in the first meeting of "The Friends of Carman Barnes" in the club-room of The Museum of Modern Art, in New York. Some of those who had been invited failed to come, and others arrived late. The room was a public one, given over to other uses; so, though I did my best under the circumstances, nothing could conceal the fact from both of us that the whole thing had been a ghastly flop. For this Miss Barnes was profoundly apologetic, taking more than her share of the blame; whereupon I suggested that we try again.

The second meeting was at the Wellesley College Club, in New York. Here we had the place to ourselves, and all the conditions were as right as could be. There were about thirty people present; the interest was intense, and another meeting was then and there arranged for a week hence, at the same time and place.

On that occasion I was fairly astride my hobby, "ready and mounted for the hot encounter," all my indifference gone. An incorrigible propagandist, here was a chance to unfold my philosophy to a class and to a generation which knew nothing of it, and, as week followed week, I enlarged the scope of the lectures, drawing heavily from books I had

written and published before many of my auditors
were born.

The next move was to Miss Barnes' large and
lofty studio on Seventy-eighth Street, taken for the
purpose, and decorated with the spoils of an ancient
Llama temple, previously exhibited at the New
York World's Fair. To our new temple of the
human spirit we gave the name of The Arch—
a bridge to span the gulf between all our yesterdays
and a future dark, dubious, but "promise crammed."
For as Nietzsche said, with the clairvoyance of incipient madness: "It would seem as though we had
before us, as a reward for all our toil, a country
still undiscovered, the horizons of which no one
has yet seen, a beyond to every country and every
refuge of the ideal that man has ever known, a
world so overflowing with beauty, strangeness,
doubt, terror, and divinity, that both our curiosity
and our lust of possession are frantic with eager-
ness."

"Our revels now are ended," but that they might
leave some "wrack behind," these talks, edited and
elaborated, are here presented, with a dedicatory
sweep of the hand to the prime-mover and provider,
Carman Barnes.

CLAUDE BRAGDON

New York, January, 1942

CONTENTS

CONTENTS

LIST OF ILLUSTRATIONS

THE ARCH LECTURES

I

EDUCATION

NOT LONG AGO I HAD OCCASION TO VISIT THE PLACE where the city and county of New York sends its insane. I found there many buildings, some of them veritable skyscrapers, all populated by madmen, idiots, the mentally unbalanced, and the people who took care of them. On my journey uptown and over the George Washington bridge, the largest single group of buildings I passed was the Medical Center, full of sick people, nurses and doctors. On my way up the East River to the World's Fair by boat, from the foot of Forty-ninth Street, the biggest building in sight was the New York Hospital; while on Welfare Island I saw hundreds of consumptives sunning themselves on the porches of pavilion after pavilion, story above story, vast in extent.

The fact that New York takes such good care of its sick and insane is indeed heartening, but is not the *magnitude* of it all significant and sinister, indicating something radically wrong with us and with our way of life? We take it all for granted, but a visitor from another planet could not help being struck by this phenomenon, and would want to know the reason for it. He might also want to know why the people he passed on the street had such worried or empty faces, and such unseeing eyes, while their children were alert and charming. How did these people get that way, and what could be done to save their children from a similar fate?

There would be great disagreement on the right answer to such a question, but my own would be that of my master, Louis Sullivan: *We have been betrayed by our education.* He felt this so deeply that he wrote a book, *Kindergarten Chats*, addressed to the young people of his day. Ostensibly it was about contemporary architecture, but it was really about education, for the buildings which he so ruthlessly dissected revealed with naked candor the consciousnesses of the men who made them; and because behind every man is an environment and an education, he examined into the nature of that education. He found that it was of the mind only, not of the will, the emotions, the imagination. It concerned itself more with facts than with underlying principles, and as Sullivan said: "To see the literal only, the physical only, the objective only, is to fail of even half-seeing, for the spiritual permeates the physical, the subjective the objective."

4

The evil results of this narrow and lop-sided system of education were written all over the buildings chosen for discussion: rooted to the spot, heavy with the spoils of vanished civilizations like criminals caught with the goods, they told the story of the survival of the evils of feudalism without its grandeurs, and the failure of democracy.

In the final chapters of his own life story, *The Autobiography of an Idea*,[1] Sullivan returns to the subject of the right kind of an education to make a success of democracy. His program corresponds so nearly to my own conception, and is so germane to the subject of this lecture, that I give it here, couched in his own winged words. Of education he says:

These things it shall do:

It shall regard the child body, the child mind, the child heart, as a trust.

It shall watch for the first symptom of surviving feudal fear and dissolve it with gentle ridicule while it teaches prudence and the obvious consequences of acts. No child that can toddle bravely is too young to know what choice means, when presented objectively and humanly. Thus it shall teach the nature of choice at the beginning.

It shall allow the child to dream, to give vent to its

[1] By permission of W. W. Norton & Company, Inc.

5

wondrous imagination, its deep creative instinct, its romance.

It shall recognize that every child is the seat of genius; for genius is the highest form of play with Life's forces.

It shall allow the precious being to grow in its wholesome atmosphere of activities, giving only that cultivation which a careful gardener gives—the children shall be the garden.

It shall utilize the fact that the child mind, in its own way, can grasp an understanding of things and ideas, supposed now in our pride of feudal thought to be beyond its reach.

It shall recognize that the child, undisturbed, feels in its own way the sense of power within it, and about it; that by intuition the child is mystic—close to nature's heart, close to the strength of Earth.

The child thus warded will be a wholesome, happy child. It will forecast the pathway to its maturity.

As from tender age the child grows into robust, demonstrative vigor, an ebullition of wanton spirits, the technic of warding will pass by degrees into the technic of training and discipline—bodily, mentally, emotionally; the imagination, the intellect, organized to work together; the process of coördination stressed. The idea of the child's natural powers will be suggested a little at a time and shown objectively.

The child by this time is passing out of its reveries; life is glowing, very real, very tangible. So shall its awakening powers be trained in the glowing real, the tangible, the three R's, made glowing and real to it as a part of its world. It is here where the difference between welcome work and a task comes into play; the difference between a manikin and a teacher.

Now arrives the stage of pre-adolescence—unromantic urge of hastening vegetative growth; the period of the literal, the bovine, disturbed at times by prophetic reverie. This is the time for literal instruction.

Now comes the stage of adolescence, when the whole being tends to deliquesce into instability, vague idealisms, emotions hitherto unknown or despised, bashfulness, false pride, false courage, introspection, impulsiveness, inhibitions, awkward consciousness of self, yet with an eye clairvoyant to that beauty which it seeks, a stirring in the soul of glory, of adventure, of romance. The plastic age of impressionability, of enthusiasms. Also the Danger Age; the age of extreme susceptibility under cover of indifference in self-protection: the age when thoughts and musings are most secret. The age that makes or breaks.

This is the crisis where democratic education, recognizing it as such, shall attain its first main objective in fixing sound character, in alert, intensive training of the native power to feel straight, to think straight, to act straight, to encourage pride in well-doing, to make so clear the moral nature of choice that the individual may realize the responsibilities involved in the consequences of choice. To train the imagination to constructive foresight, in the feeling for real things, in the uses of sentiment, of emotion, in the physical and spiritual joy of living; to stabilize the gregarious into the social sense; to set forth the dignity of the ego and of all egos.

This is the time to put on the heavy work, to utilize to the full this suddenly evolving power, the recrudescent power of instinct, to direct this power into the right channels, to prepare adolescents to become adults, free of spirit, with footing on the solid earth, with social vision clear and true.

The later technical trainings shall be imbued of the same spirit. The varied kinds all shall be set forth as specialized yet unified social activities. Science shall thus be understood and utilized, the industrial arts, the arts of applied science, and most urgently the science and art of education, all shall be understood as social functions, ministering to the all-inclusive art of creating out of the cruel feudal chaos of cross-purposes, a civilization in equilibrium, for freemen conscious of their powers, and with these powers under moral control.

Such civilization shall endure, and even grow in culture, for it shall have a valid moral foundation, understandable to all. It will possess a vigor hitherto undreamed of, a versatility, a virtuosity, a plasticity as yet unknown, for all work will be done with a living purpose, and the powers of mankind shall be utilized to the full, hence there shall be no waste.

No dream, no aspiration, no prophecy can be saner.

Man shall find his anchorage in self-recognition.

8

Here is an educational program with different objectives from the stuffing of the youthful mind with facts sufficient to pass examinations in which the pupil with the best memory is bound to come off best. There is, however, one important matter not mentioned by Mr. Sullivan in his syllabus, although—perhaps because—nearer to his heart than anything: the sense of an immanent divine: "The Great God of the Universe, this divinely-human and humanly-divine creative element and power it is my purpose to show forth." Of this immanent divine the child should be constantly reminded, rather than taught, and not by religious instruction of the ordinary sort.

Ever since William James published his famous essay, there has been much speculation about "The Moral Equivalent of War." But in a time of un-faith like the present, when the dominant religions have lost their power of appeal to the young, would it not be better to try to discover some moral equiv-alent of those ancient faiths which moved men to creative efforts and sacrificial ardors, lacking which man is just a clever, predatory animal intent mainly on destruction? Again there is need of affir-mation, on grounds unrelated to blind faith, of man's inherent divinity and transcendent destiny.

9

In my opinion the fundamental educational problem is this reawakening of God-consciousness; to make plain that "salvation" is not a religious work in the old sense, but an actual necessity of growth; that spirituality has nothing to do with conventional morality or religious emotionalism, but is an inevitable and ordained movement of the inner self toward "the world of the wondrous," and the taking of one's evolution into one's own hands.

For this, mere ethical conduct and humanitarianism—the doing of good works (modern substitutes for the old religious fervors) will not suffice. Science gives to ardent and aspiring youth but dusty answers, despite the fact that in its newest generalizations, involving the ideas of curved time and hyperspace, science stands on the very threshold of mysticism, as was predicted a quarter of a century ago by Ouspensky, in *Tertium Organum*, wherein he said: "Science must come to mysticism."

It is therefore not inconceivable that a realization of the illusory nature of time and the multi-dimensionality of space, and the dependence of both upon the evolution of perception, or consciousness, together with all the astounding implications latent in these ideas, might bridge the chasm which has existed for so long between materialism and deism, and reconcile the discoveries of Western workers with the inspired reveries of Eastern dreamers. For as C. Howard Hinton affirmed in A New Era of Thought: "Either one of two things must be true, that four-dimensional conceptions give a wonderful power of representing the thought of the East, or that the thinkers of the East must have been looking at and regarding four-dimensional existence."

How shall this body of ideas, found in the writings of such men as Hinton, Ouspensky, Dunne, and Gerald Heard, but unknown or ignored by pedagogues—ideas old as the pyramids yet fresh as paint—be brought to the attention of youth, to transform, transfigure, and revivify education from the ground up? This is a question which has preoccupied me so much that it has won me away from tasks more practical and more profitable. In his book, Design This Day, Mr. Walter Dorwin Teague says: "Mr. Bragdon is a very talented architect who forsook architecture for mysticism." This is the truth, for I have devoted these later years to writing and lecturing on this, to me, all-important subject. My readers and auditors have been for the most part women, for the reason that today in America women are not only the custodians of such culture as is ours, but they are more open to new ideas than the men of the modern world, given over, as they are, to compulsory labor, or to the transaction of sharp bargains, incredulous of things beyond their ken and outside their interests.

So when Carman Barnes told me that she had an idea for a girls' school to meet the needs of the modern young woman, I lent a willing ear, and promised to help her to the extent of trying to formulate what such a school should be "like." We would call it The Arch, because an arch is a bridge—in this case a bridge over the River of Doubt into the World of the Wondrous. Also, an arch is made up of individual stones, placed, so to speak, shoulder to shoulder, thus implying group effort and group consciousness—the coöperative as opposed to the competitive idea.

The purpose of such a school, behind and above all its other activities, would be, in Gerald Heard's phrase, "to free consciousness from accident," to prepare it for any event which might befall, and to save the pupils from that "cannibalism of the mind" which results from the purely mental approach to everything. To this end mind-culture would be mitigated by the disciplining also of the will and the emotions, so that will, heart, and mind might act together, constructively, instead of like horses pulling different ways—therefore destructively.

Because, when all is said, one is only as "good" as one's body, great attention should be devoted to its care and culture. But all physical exercises ought to be rhythmical, and not violent; coöperative, not competitive. Ensemble dancing, juggling, and acrobatics meet these conditions best, because they necessitate the absence of tension, and a correlation between the body, mind, and eye. Better than anything are the stretching exercises and the basic postures of that immemorially ancient system of self-mastery known as Yoga, and its methods of internal cleansing by means of water and air. These should be undertaken, however, only under the observation and guidance of a competent teacher, and should never be carried to great lengths—for the path of development by these means is the path of danger. Concentration and meditation should be practised daily: the stilling of the mind, and the effort to raise consciousness to higher levels of awareness.

Such a school should be conditioned by the needs of the group as a whole. True to the democratic ideal, freedom of opinion, action, and expression, should be encouraged in so far as not prejudicial to the general well-being; but all manifestations of the evil factors of vanity, self-conceit, and self-pity, unwholesome weeds in this particular garden, should be drastically dealt with.

The ultimate aim of a school of this sort would be to help its pupils to self-knowledge and self-mastery, to teach them to meet life with courage and confidence, and to acquire the power to coöperate with others in a spirit of sympathy and understanding. To compass all this, three things at least are necessary: First, the elimination of what Hinton calls "self-elements"—those blemishes known to everyone but oneself, like a smudge on the nose, to do away with which it is necessary only to become aware of it. Second, the awakening of new perceptions; and third—and most important—an ever-augmenting *rapprochement* of the personal self with the Great Self without Selfishness.

This is an ambitious program, possibly a pretentious one, but the trouble with most girls' schools is that they appear to have no ambition higher than to make those pupils who want to go to college pass the college entrance examinations, and to prepare those who do not, for social success of one sort or another. But the average young woman of today has no active desire either for what is called

14

the higher education, or for some equivalent of being "given in marriage to a noble earl who keeps a carriage." What she needs to know is how to navigate these "perilous seas forlorn"—this devastated modern world in which she finds herself.

Because it is so ambitious a program it could not be put into successful operation completely and all at once. It would be best to begin such a school in a small way, letting it grow as the plant grows, organically, searching out the human correlatives of moisture and sunlight wherever they can be found, and like the plant expanding always according to its own unique pattern—the one which I have here attempted to outline for your comment and criticism.

For this is the concern of all of you, if for no other reason than that you are women of the modern world who should know better than I how ill-fitting is the educational garment your sex has been forced to wear. There is a profound and fundamental difference between the masculine and the feminine psyche, so great that the two may be said to inhabit different worlds. Because woman is more intuitive than man, and because the intuition is the next human faculty to be developed, bringing with it an awareness of the four-dimensional world, she occupies today a position of unique, of supreme importance. But in order for her to fulfill successfully her new evolutionary function—prepared for by that freedom so instinctively fought for and so dearly won—she must be made aware of this responsibility, and man must become conscious of it, too. The situation created by this double blindness is calamitous to both, and is the cause of more unhappiness between married pairs than marital infidelity. For woman, still oppressed by that slave-psychology built up through centuries of subservience, either submits to masculine domination in the old way, trying to resist an evolutionary urge which can not but prove in the end too strong for her, or she revolts destructively. He, on his part, fearful of the loss of that supremacy which he has come to regard as his by natural right, either tightens his ancient tyranny or else encourages and incites the woman to become his sedulous ape, even to the acquiring of his characteristic masculine vices: lechery, drinking, smoking and gambling. This makes of her a creature neither man nor woman, which excites only his loathing; he has killed the thing he loves—as is the way of man, from Hamlet and Othello to the nameless hero of *The Ballad of Reading Gaol*.

To Olive Schreiner, in one of her visions, modern woman appeared in the semblance of a camel, struggling painfully to rise to its feet in order to undertake a long and necessary journey. I think you will recognize the devastating aptness of this allegory. "Women," says Emerson, "are really the heart and sanctuary of our civilization." Who but woman can bring into human life that compassion and heart-wisdom necessary to deliver man from the grip of his own destructiveness? You women should make it your business to see that the younger generation of your sex be given the kind of an education which will enable it to rise and make this necessary journey—for upon this the further evolution of the human race may depend.

II

YOGA

IT IS CLEAR THAT PRESENT-DAY EDUCATION IS NOT OF a kind calculated to meet the needs of a generation facing an imperilled, an already devastated world, since it provides no plan or pattern whereby those so educated might "out of wrecks and sediment a fairer world create." For education is almost exclusively mental, objective, factual, neglectful of that vast and mysterious demesne, the source of all beingness, the so-called subjective or subliminal self—consciousness itself, in point of fact. Modern psychology purports to deal with consciousness, but it does so mostly with regard to unhealthy, perverted, morbid manifestations; there is no organized effort, at any rate, which has as its aim the *culture* of consciousness.

We have progressed as far as we can go along the lines of purely physical evolution and technical achievement because we discover to our horror that without some corresponding evolution of consciousness—or call it conscience—this path leads to degeneracy and self-destruction. Our vitality—sapped by all sorts of diseases, and by serums to counteract them, an equilibrium of poisons—is less than that of savages; and no sooner is the conquest of the air achieved than it is employed for the extermination of human beings and the product of their labor, while with every access of technical expertness comes increased destruction—witness the present war compared with the last one. We have means but no ends, ideas but no ideals. Further evolution is impossible in a competitive society the aims of which are to inflate the ego and try to stabilize it by additions, possessions, and pretensions. To any dispassionate observer it must be plain that devolution has already begun, the signs and symptoms of degeneracy so abound. Men destroy one another because they are themselves being self-destroyed. In the convulsions of a Europe at war we have the spectacle of moral disease written large on time and space. Hitler, with his gigantic military machine, is but an agent of national and racial karma. It is significant that Madame Blavatsky, in the chapter headed "Cyclic Evolution and Karma" in *The Secret Doctrine*, published in 1888, declared that Europe was threatened with a cataclysm to which her own cycle of racial karma had led her,

19

through ways unmarked, from guilt to punishment, which are now the ways on which move onward the great European nations:

The Western Aryans had, every nation and tribe, like their Eastern brethren of the fifth race, their Golden and their Iron ages, their periods of comparative irresponsibility, or Satya age of purity, while now, several of them have reached their Iron Age [England and France she mentions particularly], the Kali Yuga, an age *Black With Horrors*. . . .

The so-called Russian Pythoness claimed that this was neither prevision or prophecy in the ordinary sense, but knowledge gained by mathematically correct computations—an understanding of the law of cycles.

How may America escape a similar fate? Not by the hoped-for Anglo-Saxon victory in the present world-war. The disease is too deep-seated, and calls for a remedy of an altogether different kind. The other day I received a letter from the Scottish chief engineer of an oil-tanker. He wrote to ask me where he could buy certain books mentioned in my autobiography. "In times like these," he said, "everyone ought to try to find a workable philosophy; hating the Germans doesn't get us anywhere."

Is there such a philosophy, and a technique for its realization in terms of a more abundant life? I think so; otherwise I should not have had the presumption to appear before you in the capacity of a teacher: to do so would be like a blind man offering to lead others, perhaps less blind, across a dangerous street. My grounds are not any self-conceived design for living; but a body of ideas and a method of self-realization, perhaps the oldest in the world. After centuries of neglect, except by isolated individuals and small and secret companies of adepts, it is here and now renascent, and for the best of reasons: it is needed in the present evolutionary crisis, being concerned with the culture of consciousness and the conquest of new worlds.

I am speaking of Yoga, that priceless jewel cherished for uncounted centuries in the brooding bosom of Asia—mother of religion, language, art—until by the operation of the law of cycles the time should come for its bestowal upon us of the West in this land destined to be the cradle of the new Sixth Race. That time is now, when we are questioning the very foundations of our knowledge, and waking up to the futility of our aims. Known about (but not known, because not practised) by informed people everywhere, it first entered the general consciousness in a big way with the publication of F. Yeats-Brown's *Lives of a Bengal Lancer,* which became a best-seller largely by reason of what it tells about Yoga—not much, but highly provocative. Then came Paul Brunton's *A Search in Secret India,* a vivid and circumstantial account of his encounters with eminent Yogins of the East. Since then there has been a deluge of Yoga books of one kind or another, the latest being Theos Bernard's *Heaven Lies within You.* Since I published my own small book, *An Introduction to Yoga,* there have been so many books on the subject that three were reviewed in a single issue of the New York *Herald Tribune's* Sunday book review section. *The Cosmopolitan* and *Harper's Bazaar* have published articles on Yoga alluringly illustrated by posturing beauties, and the *New Yorker* made it the subject of a satirical skit.

From this evidence alone it is clear that Yoga has become one of the catchwords of the day and hour, as has "space-time," and "the fourth dimension." This is passing strange when one considers the mysterious and amazing content of these expressions, and the confusion of ideas about them, even among those most informed. Stevenson said: "Mankind lives principally by catchwords," and catchwords such as these, even though uttered only for amusement or mystification, indicate some sort of a change in consciousness, a shift of interest and attention, if one compares them with the catchwords of an earlier time.

Aldous Huxley, the popular novelist, supremely scientific and cynical, was converted to the Eastern Wisdom by Gerald Heard, whose *Pain, Sex, and Time* accords to Yoga the highest praise. In *Ends and Means* Huxley reversed himself completely, for it might have been written by a Vedanta devotee. Leopold Stokowsky must have taken up Yoga as a result of his travels in India, for he told a friend that, if she would take up its practice, she would not be unhappy any more. Ruth St. Denis and Theos Bernard, Americans born and bred, found in Asia their spiritual mother just as I myself did. But it is useless to multiply examples: the point is that Yoga has profoundly influenced the thought and lives of leaders in various fields here in the West, and that the same influence is spreading and accelerating.

For this there is a reason—the one I have already stated: along the old familiar lines we have gone as far as it is possible to go. There is no salvation in the rational mind and in the life of the senses:

it is necessary to turn inward and develop what Ouspensky calls "the fourth form of the manifestation of consciousness" which brings with it mastery over time and extra-sensory perception. Yoga not only takes into account these higher states of consciousness, but provides a technique for their attainment, although to the true Yogin, bent solely on "union," the "higher powers" are in the nature of wayside flowers on the path to his true goal. For the word Yoga means to yoke, to join the personal consciousness with its higher-dimensional correlative, related to it as volume to surface, thus becoming a participator in the bliss, wisdom, and power of the universal spirit. Yoga is not an escape *from* life, but *into* life. Ouspensky calls this state or condition "the world of the wondrous," and Krishnamurti calls it "the kingdom of happiness." Although I have no more than touched its fringe, I can testify to its reality; it is not another world, but this one, experienced differently.

The adage "a little knowledge is a dangerous thing" is particularly true as regards Yoga, and if that knowledge be based upon a fundamental misconception, that danger is increased. For good or ill the word Yoga has entered the Anglo-Saxon vocabulary; if it be falsely defined or misunderstood, harm will result. I wrote *An Introduction to Yoga* more to warn than to entice. It were better never to have stepped from the easy-winding path onto that steep and stony one which leads straight upward, than for one to take up the practice of Yoga for the reason that "it gives grace and poise," as a cure for disease, or in order to gain greater power over others—for any motive, in fact, except to bind the personal self to the service of the All-Self, with everything which such surrender implies.

From the moment this first step has been taken *motive* becomes all important, for it conditions action and determines its effect. This is true to such an extent that the same action prompted by opposite motives produces opposite results, engendering widely different karmas. If the motive be for the advantage of the personal self and for its benefit solely, that self will grow ever stronger and more formidable, more difficult, therefore, to bind to the service of the higher self, which is the ultimate aim of Yoga practice—even the physical exercises and postures.

In the East, by reason of the age-old subjugation of women, Yoga has been practiced chiefly—though not exclusively—by man, woman being supposed to attain her salvation through service of him. But here the situation is different, for the women of America are in general more leisured, more cultured, more open to new ideas than men. I would even go so far as to say that women ought to practice Yoga if only to help men to that spiritual awareness and sexual control and sublimation which that practice, steadily pursued, will ultimately bring, just as she is sometimes able to interest her mate in good music and good literature because of her interest. George Meredith said that woman was the last thing civilized by man. There spoke the arrogant British male. I would say that it is the other way round, for the average American male go-getter, with his mean ambitions and his dirty mind, seems to me far less civilized than the average American woman—though it is impossible to generalize in matters of this kind.

There is also another reason why Yoga should commend itself to women. We are entering the Aquarian cycle, the Age of Woman, and in order to fulfill her great destiny it is necessary that she should develop the masculine part of her androgynous nature, but without loss of her essential *femininité*. She it is who must assume the role of initiator and guide. The practice of Yoga brings that bisexuality about, because it is one of the attributes of super-humanity—the "one far-off divine event."

This idea of the androgyne is not foreign to the thought even of materialistic science, and has always been an integral part of the loftiest religious philosophy, though concealed in symbols, and referred to only in veiled terms.

After all I have just said about the difficulties and dangers of Yoga, because it has to do with what is known as the return cycle—"that last of life for which the first was made," my recommendation of it as part of the curriculum of a girls' school may surprise you. But according to my view all life is a preparation for Yoga—*is* Yoga in some form, in point of fact—and the earlier that preparation begins the better. Such is the custom in India, where the child is encouraged to assume the lotos posture, which is easier for children than for adults. He is also taught to sit still, to close his eyes, "make a moon," and to perform simple, stretching exercises. Awareness, concentration, power of will, and ability to relax are thus developed in the child by a means of which he is scarcely conscious. Attention, reverie, and relaxation are natural to childhood. Indeed, "To find Yoga is to become as a little child." This statement is from a communication from Nancy Fullwood, author of *The Song of Sano Tarot*, given to me by her while I was engaged in writing *An Introduction to Yoga*. The whole is so simple and clear a statement of the essentials of Yoga that I used it as a fitting final summary:

Bind back to the source is Yoga. When a man loses his life to find it he has found Yoga. Make the matter so simple that a child can understand it. It will thus clarify an ancient but new truth. To become as a little child is to find Yoga.

Yoga is an important subject, and must not be hidden under signs and obscure terms, for of all simple things Yoga is the most simple. One grows into Yoga rather than attaining it through mental training, for Yoga is truly the understanding of balance. Yoga will dispel ignorance because to find Yoga is to find the source of all life. What more could you ask than Yoga?

Here is a simple illustration of Yoga: A mother ties a cord about her child, holding the ball in her hand. The child is free to run hither and yon because the wise mother lets the cord play through her fingers as far as the child desires to run. Of course the child grows up thinking that he is his own master; to tell him that his mother has him tied with a string would anger him. But when the day comes, as it surely will, when he turns his face toward his mother and sees the cord and realizes her wisdom and love, and he accepts it with joyous understanding, then he has found Yoga.

III

THE FOURTH DIMENSION

YOGA IS THE CULTURE OF CONSCIOUSNESS, A TURNING
of the attention inward, away from the world apprehensible by the senses, to gain an awareness
more immediate and more extended; it prepares for
and precipitates a higher phase of evolution. It is
vitally related to the subject of the fourth dimension, however little it may appear so, as I shall endeavor to make plain.

In that bold and brilliant challenge to modern
materialistic modes of thinking, *Tertium Organum*,
Ouspensky's chief contentions are the following:

1. That everything is consciousness of some
kind or degree.

2. That all evolution is the evolution of consciousness.

3. That the dimensionality of space depends
upon the development of consciousness, and that
space seems to us three-dimensional only because
we are in the third phase of that development—
the so-called Age of Reason; but because we have
already entered the fourth phase, which involves
the emergence of a new faculty, the intuition, those

in whom this is beginning to operate discover that space is (at least) four-dimensional. This is already foreshadowed in the theory of relativity and the concept of space-time, a four-dimensional manifold in which time is the fourth coördinate, equi-potent and interchangeable with the three known dimensions of space.

Let me see if I can make this idea of time as the fourth dimension clear. A dimension is a measure. Space is said to be three-dimensional because it is necessary to measure in three different directions, all at right angles to one another, to define the position of any point in space—the point of this pencil, for example. We measure its distance from the rear wall, the side wall, and the floor or ceiling, and we would seem to have located it with mathematical accuracy. But think a minute: we will have done so only with regard to the room, not to that larger universe of which the room—including the pencil-point—is only an infinitesimal part. For even before the measurements can be taken, the pencil-point will have undergone a complex series of changes of position by reason of the rotation of the earth on its axis—at about half the speed of a rifle bullet, the path of this planet in its journey around the sun at a velocity some forty times greater than that of a cannon-ball, and the more uncertain and vertiginous speed of the entire solar system toward its unknown goal. Now it will be plain that it is necessary to add to the three dimensions of space a fourth for the definition of position in a kinetic universe like ours—the *time* dimension, in this case the exact moment at which the measurements were taken.

To make this matter more comprehensible, I give you another example: When it is said that a certain person lives in New York, he has been located in a rough and ready kind of way as a point on the surface of a sphere. When it is added that he lives on the northwest corner of Park Avenue and Fifty-fourth Street, let us say, his position has been defined in terms of two dimensions. Now, if there is on that corner an apartment house many stories high, it is necessary to know the floor and number of his room in order to find him. This constitutes the third perpendicular, thus exhausting the three dimensions of space. But New Yorkers being notoriously peripatetic, to locate your man you must also know the *time* at which he will be at home. Again time is the fourth perpendicular—the fourth coördinate necessary to establish the position of a body in space.

31

Although this locating of a person by means of latitude, longitude, altitude, and time gives a fair idea of the sense in which time may be said to be the fourth dimension, it fails to show how time is interchangeable with the three dimensions of space, for it is thus interchangeable—all four coördinates are equipotent and homogeneous. Assuming that you have found your man on the tenth floor, say, of the apartment house—or have failed to find him —it occurs to you that you would like to know how high that floor is above the street—the length of the third perpendicular. The elevator boy, to whom you appeal for this information, naturally cannot tell you, but he happens to know that his car normally travels at a speed of five feet per second. By reference to the second hand of your watch at the moment of starting down and at the moment of stopping, you find that the elapsed time is twenty seconds, and that the distance therefore is one hundred feet. Your watch has performed the function of a tape-measure. This is a commonplace of science—all higher dynamical reasonings use motion as a translator of time into space, and space into time.

The fourth dimension is *mathematically real*, but anyone claiming physical reality for any dimensions higher than the third would be faced by this contradiction: to be physically real a thing must be only three-dimensional, three-dimensionality and materiality being in the nature of synonymous terms. "Matter is first of all three-dimensional," says Ouspensky, and with this any physicist would agree. Let me put the matter in another way: Arithmetically it is possible to raise a number to any given power; that is, to multiply it by itself any number of times. There is a known spatial correlative of the second power of a number, the square; and of its third power, the cube; but we have no direct, or sensory knowledge of that analogous form, the hypercube or tesseract—related to the cube as the cube is related to the square—which would correspond with the fourth power of a number, nor of that four-dimensional space which alone would contain it. With the geometry of such a space mathematicians have been long familiar but *is* there such a space? Is there any body for this mathematical soul?

It seems highly probable, and has such sanction as the law of analogy can give, but such are the limitations of our minds and senses that we can apprehend the fourth dimension only subjectively and bit by bit. This creates the illusion of *time*.

33

Time does not flow, it is we who are flowing, wanderers in a multi-dimensional universe. Time, as I said before, is just the same measurement of space as length, breadth, and thickness. That it seems something other is because of the limitation of our senses to three dimensions. To the extent that we are able to expand consciousness we transcend time —become what Korzybski calls "time-binders." Compared with the savage, to whom the function of a watch, a calendar, a time-table, or anything having to do with the measurement of time would be incomprehensible, we have progressed far in the matter of time-binding already, being able to predict conjunctions, eclipses, calculate the diurnal ebb and flow of the tides, and matters of that sort.

With this increasing mastery over time a psychic change is taking place in us, resulting in a new kind of awareness. The word "hunch" in the sense of an intuitive knowledge or perception has at last got into the dictionary, and the phrase "extra-sensory perception" has become part of the psychological jargon of the day and hour. This is only one of the many indications of the thinning of the veil between the three-dimensional and the four-dimensional sections of the world.

34

Though Walt Whitman probably never heard the phrase, "the fourth dimension," he had the idea in perfection, for he wrote: "I do not doubt that interiors have their interiors, and exteriors their exteriors—and that eyesight has another eyesight, and hearing another hearing, and the voice another voice." That eyesight is clairvoyance; that hearing, clairaudience; that voice, "the still, small voice of conscience," or of the Unconscious—either way you will. These inner faculties flower with the unfolding of consciousness.

In this connection let us consider what may be called the movable threshold of consciousness. Carl du Prel says, in his *Philosophy of Mysticism*:

From the standpoint of every animal organism we can divide external nature into two parts, which are the more unequal as the organic grade is lower. The one includes that part with which the sense apparatus establishes relations, the other is transcendental for the organism in question; that is, the organism lives in no relation to it. In the biological process the boundary line between these two world-halves has been pushed continually, forward in the same direction. The number of senses has increased, and their functional ability has risen. . . . The biological rise and the rise of consciousness thus signify a constant removal of the boundary between representation and reality at the cost of the transcendental part of the world, and in favor of the perceived part.

Now if this shifting psycho-physical threshold is simply the dividing line between lower and higher spaces, then the whole evolutionary process consists in the conquest, dimension by dimension, of related space-worlds. This certainly holds true as far as our observation extends: To the grub, working its way up to the surface of the earth, that surface is transcendental; to the caterpillar, the earth is real, and the free air transcendental; while to the butterfly, master of this added dimension, the threshold has again receded. Indeed, there are indications that the butterfly is in possession of a space sense which is still a mystery to us. Fabre himself could not explain how the great peacock moth was able to find its mate in the dark and at a distance sometimes of miles.

Arguing by analogy, everything which is to us transcendental exists nevertheless in some space. It is therefore possible that by an intention of consciousness upon it, we may be able first to apprehend, and then to perceive as real, that which is now considered transcendental. Right at this point we cross the track of Plato. In one of the Socratic

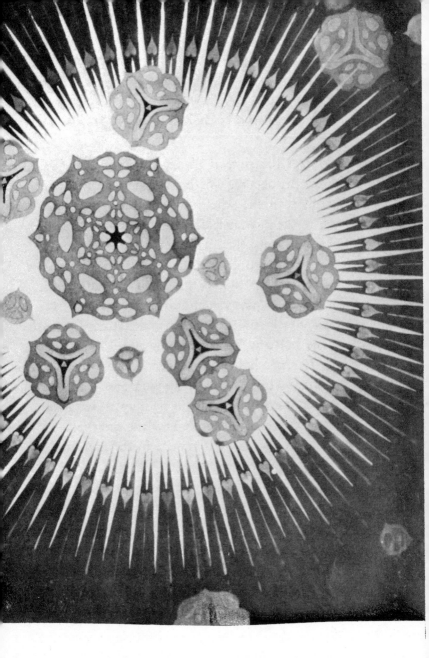

Design by Claude Bragdon, suggested by the retinal
images seen after looking at the sun.

dialogues Socrates makes an experiment upon a slave who is standing by. He causes space perceptions to awaken in the mind of the slave by directing his close attention to some simple geometrical diagrams traced in the sand. Plato's comment was that behind the mental awakening exhibited in Meno's slave there was a vast, an infinite perspective. It is possible that by dwelling on elementary higher-space concepts we may repeat Socrates' experiment on new grounds; and by an intention of consciousness upon the fourth dimension we may push back the psycho-physical boundary and capture for sense the now transcendental fourth dimension.

Because this pushing back of this threshold is incessant and universal, we have only to observe its lower and earlier manifestations in order to understand something of its immediate and ultimate. Such observation leads to the conclusion that our sense of time may be only an imperfect sense of space. This is clear if we consider the manner in which the facts of space must present themselves to a consciousness with a less developed space-sense than ours—and by a less developed sense of space is meant a more limited power of representation in terms of form. Many things which we as human beings apprehend without difficulty *simultaneously*, after the manner of space, such a consciousness could only apprehend *successively*, after the manner of time. A worm, for example, requires time in order to examine an angle or a hole, or the floor upon which we look down—things in which with us the time-element does not enter at all. Thus, that which is *time* to one grade of consciousness is *space* for the next ascending grade. The fourth dimension cannot manifest itself to our three-dimensional powers of perception as space; therefore, it becomes apprehensible as time—that is, as changes of state in the objects of our world, such changes involving a temporal element—as life, growth, organic being, *phenomena*, in point of fact. One manner of conceiving of the fourth dimension, therefore, is as *time-changes*.

This pushing back of the psycho-physical threshold is the next evolutionary step, and cannot be left to chance, but must be consciously undertaken, under penalty of devolution if this be not done. It is difficult, because those materialistic and mechanistic concepts of the world, which we have been taught to believe, have cut us off from contact with reality; and if illusions are made to seem real, reality, when experienced, will seem like an illusion. The exercise of mental cleverness and dexterity, and the seeking of merely sensuous gratifications have so sealed up the essential self that people suffer a kind of strangulation of consciousness, and become highly dualistic, the submerged self breaking out now and then, and always destructively, not creatively, according to its essential nature.

More than our lives depend upon the making of this effort to go forward, taking our evolution in our own hands. For the struggle for mastery between the blind and unconscious forces of materialism—showing themselves as greed and fear—and those beneficent forces, now pressing into life through those who are able to respond to them, is even now upon us. All conflicts between nations, races, classes, must now be interpreted in terms of this greater warfare between what Ouspensky calls "the two races of men"—those who are capable of attaining, through individual effort, to the fourth form of the manifestation of consciousness (bringing an awareness of the four-dimensional world), and those who do not or can not make that effort. This is a conflict in which the minority for whom "there shall be time no longer" will either conquer or disappear from the lighted stage of phenomenal life, with everything to be done over again in some far-distant cycle.

The best preparation I know for this conflict—personal or world wide, inner or outer—is the daily practice of Yoga, the exercise of the mind and imagination upon four-dimensional concepts, and the opening of the door of the heart to everything and everyone. And always remember while so engaged, that there are no dimensions, no time, no space, but only consciousness, which evokes them, becoming by these means aware of itself and of its essential divinity. Dimensions are but the rungs of the ladder whereby we mount to the conception of infinity; our sense of space is the assurance that we abide in God; our sense of time, that He abides in us. Both are but modes of consciousness, just as Kant said—growing, expanding modes.

It may be asked what all this has to do with the idea of a school of a new type, which we are here to consider. This is my answer: Every great school of the past inculcated some attitude toward life—a philosophy, a point of view. This thing may be compared to the·digit before a row of ciphers (by which I mean the subjects studied), which alone gives them value, lacking which they are *nothing*.

A school without some sort of ideal, a school which enthrones the mind, and by ignoring it denies the power of the spirit, is to my mind just that—nothing multiplied by nothing. The school here envisioned would be founded on Yoga, an ancient verity which affirms the power of the spirit; on the concept of higher space, which justifies the Yoga philosophy on entirely new grounds, and on the sovereignty of love in all of the affairs of life as taught by Jesus Christ.

IV

SYMBOLS AND SACRAMENTS

IT IS SIGNIFICANT—EVEN IRONICAL—THAT THE MATE-
rialistic point of view, which found its sanction in
nineteenth-century science, should stand today discredited by the penetration of a newer science into
a world where matter loses its meaning, where time
is swallowed up in space-time, where form is only
the shadow-play of forces masquerading as forms,
and where forces, it may be, are only the shadow-
play of a conscious intelligence which for lack of a
better name we call the Unconscious—not because
it is unconscious, but because for the most part *we*
are unconscious of *it*.

Here at last we have an arch which can bridge
the chasm separating Western workers and Eastern
dreamers, and a fulfillment of Ouspensky's prophecy that science must come to mysticism. The
greatest need today is some inspiring view of life
in which it is possible to believe, and a technique of
living which shall be in accordance with it. In Yoga
we have the most ancient religious philosophy vin-
dicated by the newest discoveries in psychology and
physics, for the higher space theory justifies, by im-

plication, a faith in evolutionary possibilities hitherto undreamed of, and Yoga provides a workable method for taking one's evolution into one's own hands. Other ingredients for a moral equivalent of the old religions are, however, needed, and it is about one of these which I propose now to speak.

The coming time will have need of another and a richer language than the spoken and written word, and a reading of earth and an interpretation of life in terms of that new language. The old religions had such a language in their symbols and sacraments—indeed, it may almost be said that they had no other—but to us of today this is dead language. Symbolism, and the habit of thought which it engenders, is, however, too precious a thing not to be made our own; but how shall this be accomplished?

First, let us examine into the habit of mind which will yield that new language of which we are in search. Fundamentally it consists of looking upon nature as an arras embroidered over with the images and symbols of the things it conceals from view— the spiritual and metaphysical aspect of everything. Emerson voiced the right attitude when he said, "I believe that hints and telegraphic signals are arriving to me, every moment, out of the interior eternity. I am tormented with impatience to make them out." We are ourselves symbols dwelling in a world of symbols—a world many times removed from that ultimate reality to which all things bear figurative witness. For the commonest thing has yet some mystic meaning, and ugliness and vulgarity dwell only in the unillumined mind.

What mystic meaning, it may be asked, is contained in such things as a brick, a house, a hat, a pair of shoes? A brick is the ultimate atom of a building; a house is that larger body which man makes for his uses, just as his Self has built its habitation of flesh and bones; hat and shoes are felt and leather insulators with which we shut ourselves off from those beneficent and health-giving currents which would flow into us and through us from the air and from the earth. It may be objected that these answers only substitute for the lesser symbol a greater, but this is inevitable; if for the greater symbol were named one still more abstract and inclusive, the ultimate verity would be as far from affirmation as before. For there is nothing of which the mind can conceive which is not a symbol of something greater and higher than itself.

The dictionary defines a symbol as "something that stands for something else and serves to represent it, or to bring to mind one or more of its qualities." Now this world is a reflection of a higher world (the astral), and that of a higher world still (the mental), and so on. Everything, indeed, is a symbol of something higher, since by reflecting, it stands for, and serves to represent it. And the thing symbolized, being itself a reflection, is itself a symbol. By countless repetitions of this reflecting process throughout the many planes (sub-planes and super-planes) of nature, each thing becomes a symbol not of one thing only, but of many, all intimately correlated, and this is the reason for those underlying analogies, those "secret subterranean passages between matter and soul" which have ever been the preoccupation of the poet and the mystic, but which some day may become the serious preoccupation of scientific men.

Let us briefly pass in review the various terms of such an ascending series of symbols: members of one family, they might be called, since they follow a single line of descent.

Gold, as a thing by itself, without any relation to symbolism, is a metallic element, having a characteristic yellow color, very heavy, very soft, the most ductile, malleable, and indestructible of metals. In its minted form it is the life-force of the body economic, since on its abundance and free circulation the prosperity of everyone depends; it is that for which men and nations strive and contend. This, then, is gold in its first and lowest symbolical aspect: a life-principle, a motive force in human affairs. But it is not gold which has gained for man his lordship over nature; it is fire, the yellow gold not of the earth but of the air. Cities and civilizations, arts and industries, have ever followed the camp-fire of the pioneer. Sunlight comes next in sequence—sunlight, which focused in a burning glass spontaneously produces flame. The world subsists on sunlight; all animate creation grows by reason of it and languishes without it, just as prosperity waxes or wanes with the supply of gold. The magnetic force of the sun, specialized as *prana*—breath —fulfills the same function in the human body as does gold in civilization, sunlight in nature: its abundance and free flow make for health, its dearth for enervation. Higher than *prana* is the mind, that Promethean gift whereby man menaces Jove himself and his hierarchy of lesser gods. Higher than the mind is the heart, and a "heart of gold" is one warmed and lighted by love. Highest of all is the desire of the spirit, which no human love satisfies, but Truth only, the Golden Person, the Light of the World—the very Godhead itself.

Thus there is earthy, airy, etheric gold; gold as intellect, gold as love, gold as truth: from the curse of the world, the cause of crimes without number, there ascends a Jacob's Ladder of symbols to divinity itself, whereby man may learn that God works by sacrifice, that His universe is itself His broken body. For as gold in the purse, fire on the hearth and in the forge, sunlight for the eyes, breath in the body, knowledge in the mind, and wisdom in the understanding, He draws all men unto Him, and even when they flee Him, His are the wings:

When me they fly, I am the wings.

Keeping this first sequence clearly in mind, let us now trace another, parallel to it: the feminine, of which the first may be considered the corresponding masculine. Silver is a white, ductile, metallic element. In coinage it is a synonym for ready cash— gold in the bank is silver in the pocket; hence, silver may be said to be the reflection, or second power of gold. Just as ruddy gold is correlated with fire, so is pale silver with water; and as fire is of and from the sun, so do the waters of the earth follow the moon in her courses. The golden sun, the silver moon: these commonly employed adjectives themselves supply the correlation. Another index of its validity is that one of the properties of water is its power of reflecting, and moonlight is reflected sunlight. If gold is the mind, silver is the body, in which the mind is imaged; if gold is flame-like love, silver is brooding affection; and if gold and the sun stand for truth, silver and the moon stand for beauty— the form-side, or feminine aspect of truth.

There are two forces always and everywhere operative, one of projection, the other of recall. Nature, with tireless ingenuity, everywhere publishes this fact: in bursting bud and falling leaf, in the up-drawn waters and the descending rain. Throw a stone into the air and when the initial impulse is exhausted, gravity brings it to earth again. In human society these centrifugal and centripetal forces find expression in the anarchic and radical spirit which breaks down and re-forms existing institutions, and the conservative spirit which preserves and upbuilds by gradual accretion; they correspond to aqueous igneous action in the formation of the earth itself, and find their prototypes also in man and woman. These two symbolize forces centrifugal and centripetal, not only in their essential natures and in their difference of function, but in their physical aspects and peculiarities as well, for man is small of flank and broad of shoulder, with relatively large extremi-

48

ties—*centrifugal*, that is—while woman has broad hips, narrow shoulders, and small feet and hands—*centripetal*. Woman's instinctive and unconscious gestures are *toward* herself, man's *away from* himself.

It might be held that the anatomical differences between the sexes result solely from their difference of function with regard to the reproduction and conservation of the race, and there is plenty to justify such a view, but the one truth does not necessarily exclude the other. As Chesterton well said: "Something in the evil spirit of our time forces people always to have found some material and mechanical explanation." Such would have us believe, with Schopenhauer, that the lover's delight in the beauty of his mate dwells solely in his instinctive perception of her fitness to be the mother of his child. This is undoubtedly a factor in the glamour woman casts on man, but there are other factors, higher as well as lower, corresponding to different aspects of our manifold nature. First of all, there is mere physical attraction: to man physical woman is a cup of potential delight; but just as he fecundates her body so does she fecundate his imagination, inspiring him to pursue the highest that is in him, giving point to the saying that a man's star is always connected to a woman's garter. Higher than physical is emotional love whereby woman appeals to man by reason of her maternal tenderness and her need for protection. On the mental plane his masculine reason would supplement itself with her feminine intuition; he recognizes in her a projection of his own soul, the bride of his spirit, while the slumbering god in him perceives her to be that portion of himself, put forth before the world was, to be the mother not alone of human children, but of all those myriad forms, within which entering, "as in its sheath a knife," he becomes the Enjoyer, realizing vividly and concretely his bliss, his wisdom, and his power.

Adam and Eve, and the tree in the midst of the Garden! After man and woman a tree is perhaps the most universal and significant symbol: every tree is the Tree of Life in the sense that it is a representation of universal becoming. Rooted in the earth, its mother, and nourished by her juices, it strives ever upward to its father, the sun. All things grow as a tree grows, from unity to multiplicity, from simplicity and strength to complexity and fineness. We love and understand the trees because we have ourselves passed through their evolution, and they survive in us as the arterial and nervous systems, the roots of one in the heart, the other in the brain. Has not the body its trunk, bearing aloft the head like a flower—a cup to hold the precious juices of the brain? And has not that trunk its tapering limbs which ramify into hands and feet, fingers and toes, like twigs and branches?

Closely related to symbolism is sacramentalism. A sacrament is a ceremony or act regarded as an outward and visible sign of an inward and spiritual grace. The sacramental life consists in habitually perceiving an ulterior meaning and significance in the acts and events of every day; though binding us to a sensuous existence, these nevertheless contain within themselves the power of emancipating us from it: over and above their immediate use, their pleasure or their profit, they have a hidden meaning with some message well for us to understand.

A classic example of a sacrament is the Holy Communion of the Christian Church: On the evening of the night on which He was to be betrayed, Jesus and His disciples were gathered together at the feast of the Passover. Aware of His impending betrayal, passion, and death, and desirous of impressing powerfully upon His chosen followers the nature and purpose of His sacrifice, Jesus enacted a sacrament with the simple materials of the repast: He took bread and broke it, and gave a piece to each of them as a symbol of His broken body, and to each He passed a cup of wine as a symbol of His poured-out blood. In this act, as in the washing of His disciples' feet on the same occasion, He made His ministrations to the needs of men's bodies an allegory of His greater ministration to the needs of their souls.

The Sacrament of the Lord's Supper is of such beauty and power that it has persisted even to the present day. It lacks, however, the element of universality—at least by other than Christians its universality would be denied. Let us seek, therefore, something more all-embracing to illustrate the sacramental view of life.

Marriage is the public avowal of love between a man and a woman; their assumption of its attendant privileges, duties, and responsibilities are matters so pregnant with consequences to them and to the race that the sacramental character of marriage is felt and acknowledged by right-thinking people, even though some of them would be puzzled to know the reason why.

The reason is revealed in the answer to the question: of what is marriage a symbol? The best answer is found in the well-known doctrine, common to every religion, of the spiritual marriage between God and the soul—the higher self and the lower. What Christians name "The Mystic Way," and Buddhists, "The Path," comprise those changes of consciousness through which every soul passes on its upward journey. When the personal life is conceived of as an allegory of this inner, more intense life of the spirit, it assumes a sacramental character. With surprising unanimity the followers of different religions have given the name of marriage to that memorable moment in "the flight of the alone to the Alone" when the soul, after trials and purgations, enters into indissoluble union with the spirit, or "bridegroom," that divinely creative principle whereby it is made fruitful for the world. Marriage, then, however dear and close the union, is the sacrament of a union dearer and closer, for it is the fair prophecy that on some higher arc of the evolutionary spiral the soul will be initiated into divine mysteries of which the transports of lovers in one another's arms are but faint and far foretaste.

As an example of the power of symbols and sacraments to induce those changes of consciousness leading to liberation, it is said that an eminent scientist was moved to alter his habit of thought and mode of life on reflecting, while in his bath one morning, that though each day he was at such pains to make clean his body, he made no similar purgation of his mind and heart. The idea impressed him so profoundly that he began practising the higher cleanliness from that day forth.

If it be true, as I believe, that ordinary life in the world is a training for a life more real and more sublime which may be entered at any moment, then everything pertaining to life in the world can possess —does possess—a symbolical and sacramental meaning, becomes a door into that more real world, in point of fact.

When at the end of a cloudy day the sun bursts forth in splendor and sets red in the west, it is a sign to the weather-wise of fair weather on the morrow. But to the devotee of the sacramental life it holds a richer promise: to him the sun is a symbol of his own divine nature; the clouds, those worldly preoccupations which have interfered with its shining. This purely physical phenomenon, therefore, which brings to others a scarcely noticeable increase of warmth and light and an indication of fair weather, induces in him an ineffable sense of divine immanence. When the sacramentalist goes swimming in the sea, he enjoys to the full the

54

attendant physical exhilaration, but a greater joy flows from the realization that he has gone back to his great Sea-Mother—that feminine principle of which the sea is the perfect symbol, since water brings all things to birth and nurtures them. When, going to bed at night, he lays aside his clothes—that two-dimensional sheath of his three-dimensional body, it is in full assurance that his body in turn will be abandoned by his inwardly-retreating consciousness, and that he will travel wherever he wills in his subtle four-dimensional body, related to the physical body as that is related to the clothes which he has just laid aside.

To every sincere seeker Nature reveals her secrets, but because men differ in their curiosities she reveals different things to different men. All are rewarded for their devotion in accordance with their interests and desires, but woman-like, Nature gives herself most freely to the most ardent wooer. This favored lover is the mystic: forever seeking the spiritual content of everything, he sees in Nature a book of symbols capable of being interpreted in terms of the sacramental life. In the reverent study of animal and insect life, he gains hints of what he is and what he may become—something analogous to the grub, a burrowing thing; to the caterpillar, a crawling thing; and finally to the butterfly, a radiant winged creature. In time this sort of reading of earth becomes a settled habit, and one day he experiences its rich rewards.

V

THE MAGIC AND MYSTERY OF NUMBER

MY LAST DISCOURSE WAS ABOUT A LANGUAGE OF symbols, more eloquent for the expression of a certain order of ideas than is the spoken or the written word. Mathematics, too, is a language, perhaps the most perfect and potent that there is. For although a necessary concomitant of the sharp bargain, the chemical experiment, and indeed the scaffolding which makes possible the manifold activities of everyday life, the gift of mathematics is primarily to the mind and spirit. It is useful not alone for helping us out of our physical predicaments, but for conveying truths incapable of such clear expression in any other way. Geometry and number were so used by Pythagoras in his famous school at Crotona, and I like to cherish the idea that in a former life I was a pupil in that school, so preoccupied have I always been with numbers because of the profound meanings I fancy that I find in them.

Consider this paradox: mathematics, the very thing common sense swears by and dotes on, contradicts common sense at every turn. Common sense balks at the idea of *less than nothing*, yet the minus quantity, which in one sense is less than nothing in that something must be added to it to make it equal to nothing, is a concept without which algebra would have come to a full stop. Again, the science of quaternions, in which the progress of electrical science is essentially involved, embraces (explicitly or implicitly) the extensive use of imaginary or impossible quantities of the earlier algebraists. The very words, "imaginary" and "impossible," are eloquent of the defeat of common sense in dealing with concepts with which it can not practically dispense. For the moment, common sense balks at the idea of a fourth dimension, a direction definitely at right angles to every known direction of our space— to common sense a thing clearly impossible and absurd. Meantime the mathematician, to whom such a conception is mathematically sound, and to whom the fourth power of a number is no less "real" than its third (the cube), is at home with the idea of a space of four dimensions, and speculative philosophy is building for the spirit of man statelier mansions there.

The Promethean fire of mathematics lights up ever new horizons, and its achievements in the past one hundred years give to thought the very freedom which it seeks; but mathematics is not most itself, but least so, when, immersed in the manifoldness of phenomenal life, it is made to serve purely utilitarian ends. So I shall ask you to look at numbers in a way to which you are unaccustomed—the Pythagorean way—and to consider their magic and their mystery, because the more one studies them the more magical and mysterious do they appear.

First of all, let us conceive of the numbers as proceeding from unity towards infinity in groups or families expressed by the multiplication table. Each group would be related to the digits in such a way that the number seven, for example, would be number one of the family of sevens, fourteen its two, twenty-one its three, and so on; in the same way that three, six, nine, and twelve would be the one, two, three, and four of the family of threes.

Next, single out what I shall call "conjunctive" numbers, which are those whereby the members of different "families" enter into relation with one another. These numerical conjunctions may be compared to astronomical conjunctions, whereby the planets, revolving around the sun at different speeds and in widely separated orbits, come at certain times and places in line with one another, when they are said to be in conjunction. We discover that twelve is the first important conjunctive number, because in a series of twos it is the sixth, of threes the fourth, of fours the third, and of sixes the second. Eleven and thirteen are not conjunctive numbers because the members of other families do not meet in them in just this way; fourteen is so in a series of twos and of sevens. The next conjunctive number after twelve of three and four and their first multiples is twenty-four, and the next, thirty-six—the two and three of a family of twelves.

It is evident that this matter of numerical conjunctions consists merely in resolving numbers into their prime factors and that a conjunctive number is a common multiple, but to name it so and then dismiss the subject as known and exhausted shows a lack of imagination causing one to miss the wonder and beauty of it all—an impression analogous to that made by the swift-moving balls of a juggler, the evolutions of drilling troops, or the intricate figures of an ensemble dance. These things are number, concrete and animate in time and space, just as music is arithmetic made audible, and architecture, geometry made visible.

Numbers have sex: are masculine or feminine. Such was the teaching of the Egyptian hierophants from whom Pythagoras derived his philosophy of numbers. Odd numbers were conceived of as masculine, or generative; and even numbers as feminine, or parturient, because of their divisibility. Harmonious combinations were those involving the marriage of a masculine and a feminine number—an odd number and an even. It is interesting to note in this connection that in music the principal consonant intervals within the octave are expressible by ratios consisting of an odd number and an even, with a difference of 1 between them: $1 : 2$, the octave; $2 : 3$, the major fifth; $3 : 4$, the major fourth; $4 : 5$, the major third; and $5 : 6$, the minor third. The same idea of the sex of numbers prevailed in Europe during the Middle Ages, perhaps by reason of the close affinity between Freemasonry and the Egyptian wisdom, for three strokes of the church-bell announced the death of a man, and two strokes that of a woman.

Whether or not one believes that numbers are masculine or feminine, there is a fundamental and deep-seated difference between odd numbers and even. I learned this when I used to practice juggling tennis balls. With an odd number they had to be tossed into the air with one hand and caught in the other, but with an even number each ball had to be caught by the hand from which it was thrown. A similar difference holds in the case of magic square formation; the rules governing odd-number and even-number magic squares are necessarily different, because even-number squares have no central cell. For a third instance, the difference between three-four time and common time in music is basic.

From the Pythagorean point of view, numbers not only have sex-differentiation, but they have individuality, each one of the digits having a character and "meaning all its own." Furthermore, in our universe, which is said to be "septenary," each of the first seven digits is associated with one of the seven colors of the spectrum, one of the seven notes of the diatonic musical scale, and one of the seven "rays" representing cosmic forces. First-ray activity is said to be of the will; second-ray, of the heart (Love-Wisdom); third-ray, of the intelligence. The fourth ray is supposed to make for balance and harmony. The Pythagoreans regarded five as the marriage number, since it is made up of the first masculine and the first feminine numbers (two and three), and more particularly because five expresses the length of the hypotenuse of a right-angled triangle, the sides of which are respectively three and four. Further than this I shall not go.

Associated with every one of the digits is a geometrical form or symbol—sometimes several of them

—expressive of it: nothingness, yet the womb of all things is the circle; the monad, one, is symbolized by a vertical line. That line within the circle, bisecting it, yields the dyad, two. Three is the trefoil, or the triangle; four is represented by the square or by the cross. Five is the pentagon, or the five-pointed star; six corresponds to two intersecting equilateral triangles forming the so-called Shield of David, or Solomon's Seal. Seven can be represented by the double-armed cross, made up of seven equal linear units, three vertical and four horizontal, or by a nest of seven circles tangential to one another. Such symbols reveal the *nature* of a number.

Such graphic correlatives of numbers paint their portrait, as it were, revealing their uniqueness and their inherent beauty. For this purpose such graphic symbols are superior to the familiar Arabic notation, which, however admirable for purposes of computation, is of too condensed and arbitrary a character to reveal the properties of individual numbers. To state, for example, that four is the first square and eight the first cube conveys no clear idea to the non-mathematical mind, but if four be represented as a square made up of four smaller squares, and eight by a cube made up of eight smaller cubes, the fact is apprehended instantly and without effort.

Numbers proceed from unity toward infinity and return again to unity, as the soul, defined by Pythagoras as a self-moving number, goes forth from, and returns to the Unmanifest—to God. These two acts, one of projection, the other of recall, these two forces, centrifugal and centripetal, are symbolized in the operations of addition and subtraction. Within them is embraced the whole of computation; but because every aggregation of units is itself a unit, capable of being added or subtracted, there are the operations of multiplication and division, which are the addition and subtraction of groups, so to speak.

Number is the "first form of Brahm," the inner essence of all things, the shape of things past and things to come; it lurks in the heartbeat and is blazoned forth on the starred canopy of night. Substance in a state of vibration—that is, conditioned by number—undergoes those myriad transformations which constitute phenomenal life. Elements separate and combine chemically according to fixed numerical ratios, crystallization takes place according to fixed angles: "Moon, planet, gas, crystal, are concrete geometry and number," just as Emerson has said.

There are no more conspicuous examples of the mystery and magic of number than are to be found in those numerical acrostics known as magic squares. A magic square is a progression of numbers arranged in square form in such a manner that those in each band, vertical and horizontal, as well as the two diagonals, shall add up to the same sum. Though classed a mathematical recreation, magic squares have engaged the serious attention of certain great minds—Benjamin Franklin's among them—and from antiquity religious or mystical significance has been attached to them. They are of unknown and ancient origin. One is cut on the stone lintel of the gate of the old fort at Gwalior, in India. Engraved on precious stones or metal, they are still worn in the East as talismans or amulets, being supposed to possess magical properties.

Albrecht Dürer introduced one of the most remarkable four by four squares in existence into his famous engraving "Melancholia." Here it is:

16	3	2	13
5	10	11	8
9	6	7	12
4	15	14	1

Dürer's "Melancholia" Magic Square
1514

It is known that the Melancholia was engraved in 1514, and it is interesting to note that the two cen-

65

ter numbers of the bottom row of the magic square taken together form 1514.

In this square not only do all the vertical, all the horizontal, as well as the two diagonal rows yield the magic sum of thirty-four, but also the four corner cells as well as the four center cells. Or go around the square clockwise: the first cell beyond the first corner, plus the first cell beyond the second corner, plus the first cell beyond the third corner, plus the first beyond the fourth, equals thirty-four. If the square be divided into four lesser squares by means of axial lines at right angles to one another, every one of the four squares of numbers of four numbers formed in this manner also yields the magic sum of thirty-four. Or take any number at random: find the three other numbers corresponding to it in any manner with respect to the two axial lines and the sum of these four numbers will be thirty-four!

Notwithstanding the amazing intricacy of these numerical relations, the manner of formation of this square is extremely simple. It was shown me by Mr. Royal V. Heath, the author of the book called *Mathemagics*. Here is his method:

First place the numbers from one to sixteen consecutively in the form of a square as shown in Figure 1.

Second, leave the diagonals untouched, interchange the two numbers in the top row (15 and 14) *not in the diagonals* with the two numbers in the bottom row (3 and 2) *not in the diagonals*, as in Figure 2.

Third, interchange the two numbers in the first column (9 and 5) *not in the diagonals*, and lastly likewise interchange the two numbers (12 and 8) in the fourth column *not in the diagonals*, as in Figure 3, and you have the Dürer square.

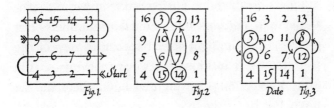

Fig. 1. Fig. 2. Date Fig. 3.

A square of numbers arranged in so-called magical formation may be said to have undergone a kind of *polarization*, making it as different from any fortuitous arrangement of numbers in square form as a horseshoe magnet is different from a horseshoe. The distinguishing thing about a magic square is equipoise, balance, polarity. May not this amazing transformation of a simple arithmetical progression contain within it a suggestion of some analogous "Great Work" capable of being wrought within the confused and chaotic nature of man through the operation of his will and intelligence—some power over the forces and factors of his life which would enable him to operate at all times with his entire nature instead of with unrelated parts of it, feebly and fragmentarily, and by a balance of positive and negative, effort and relaxation, action and counter-action, attain that "liberation" longed for by everyone?

This may seem a far-fetched comparison—perfected man and a perfected square of numbers—but it is less so than might at first appear, in view of the fact that man is himself a square, having, as the great Kepler long ago pointed out, "the same six limits as the cube has, most perfectly marked," his height being equal to the spread of his outstretched arms. Perfected man is androgynous—it is this which constitutes his perfection. I shall now show you a magic square of four by four made up of two orders of counting: the ordinary order, therefore prime, therefore masculine; and the reverse-ordinary, therefore derivative, therefore feminine.

In this square, which represents a "marriage" between these two orders of counting, the numbers of the masculine order are arranged in the form of a diagonal cross, and of the feminine order in the form of a circle, together forming the male-female symbol, the "rose" and the "cross," a Rosicrucian symbol for perfected man.

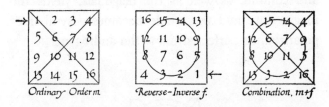

Ordinary Order m. Reverse-Inverse f. Combination, m+f

It is first necessary to set down the first sixteen numbers in their ordinary order—from right to left and downward—in the shape of a square, as above. The two sets of numbers indicated by the diagonal lines add up to thirty-four, the magic sum, and must therefore be retained, and in this position, since they constitute the diagonals of the finished magic square. Next, form another square of numbers, similar in all respects to the first one except that instead of beginning at the upper left hand corner and writing downward, in the ordinary manner, one does the exact opposite: begins, that is, at the lower right hand corner and proceeds to the left and upward—the obverse-reverse ordinary order, to give it a name.

Next one substitutes for the four pairs of numbers in the original square not contained in the diagonals, the four in this square indicated by the circular line, in their corresponding positions. Now the original square has become a magic square, for every row and column, as well as the diagonals, yields the magic sum, and the whole becomes a symbol of polarized, or perfected man—the androgyne.

VI

ARCHETYPES

THE DICTIONARY DEFINITION OF AN ARCHETYPE IS "original model." This is correct as far as it goes, but it does not go far enough. It ought to take us into the fourth dimension, because the archetype of a thing is its four-dimensional correlative. Could we realize this clearly, it might give us a better understanding of the nature of phenomenality as the result of the intersection of our world with a higher dimensional world, its higher dimensions assuming to our limited perceptions the aspect of time, change, causality.

Let me try to make this clearer by the familiar device of reducing everything one "space" and dramatizing the way the things of our world would appear to a flatlander—the denizen of a two-dimensional space. Imagine a world of two dimensions in the semblance of a pool of water covered by a film, or scum, which would represent the matter of that world. Next observe the intrusion of some three-dimensional object—an archetype, in point of fact—into his film world as it would appear to the plane-man, who has the sense of the two dimensions of that world, but lacks the sense of the third dimension—the one perpendicular to his plane—which would constitute for him "higher" space.

Assume the object in question to be a sphere: its first contact with the film would be as a point, expanding into a circle. This would attain a maximum diameter equal to that of the sphere, after which the circle would shrink again to a point and disappear. All of these modifications of form would be caused by the increasing involvement of the sphere into his world, and the third or vertical dimension of the sphere would register to the plane-man as *time*. He could apprehend this spatial dimension only as temporal duration—the time it took the sphere to immerse itself. The disturbances and displacements of the matter of his film world, and the expanding and diminishing form traced therein, all caused by the transit of a (to him) higher dimensional object, would constitute a phenomenon, although in that object itself there would have been no change: it did not begin its existence when it entered the film, nor end when the transit was accomplished. Although the generator of many plane cross-sections of itself, none of these represented its true, or archetypal form, but only the lower-dimensional correlative of it.

Now raise everything one space: the film world becomes our world of three dimensions, the three-dimensional world becomes the four-dimensional, impossible of apprehension by us save through the three-dimensional tracings which appear as forms changing in time—as phenomena. This may give some idea of my own concept of an archetype, a "form of all forms," one might call it. Each one of us has his archetypal, or four-dimensional body, which persists from birth to death—and before birth and after death. Ouspensky, in *Tertium Organum*, says of this archetypal body, called *linga sharira* in Oriental philosophy:

The four-dimensional body is the infinite number of *moments of existence* of the three-dimensional one—its states and positions. The three-dimensional body which we see appears as a single figure—one of a series of pictures on a cinematographic film, as it were. . . . Eastern philosophy regards the body as something *impermanent* which is in a condition of perpetual interchange with its surroundings. The particles come and go. After one second the body is already not absolutely the same as it was one second before. Today it is in a considerable degree not what it was yesterday. After seven years it is *quite a different body*. But despite all this, something always persists from birth to death, changing its aspect a little, but remaining the same.

73

This is the *linga sharira*. But if we try to represent to ourselves mentally the image of a man from birth to death, with all the peculiarities and traits of childhood, manhood and senility, as if extended in time, that would be the *linga sharira*.

An archetype is an *essence*, and in dwelling upon that word think, if you please, of the meaning of *essential*, for the archetype of anything is that which is essential to it, that which makes it what it is—without which, indeed, it could not exist at all. Itself invariable, it is the cause and source of every variation; these inhere within it in the same sense in which the circle, the ellipse, the parabola, and the hyperbola inhere within the cone. They are every one *conic sections*, and the cone may be considered the archetype of them all.

But mathematics aside—so clarifying a thing to some minds and so confusing to others—consider the matter of archetypes rather in this way: If we take any solid object (other than a sphere) and hold it so that it casts a shadow of itself on an illuminated surface, as it is turned about in the hand, the shadow takes a different shape with each change of position. The object itself is unalterably *one*, but its projections upon a plane are many and various, sometimes resembling one another not at all. Each shape the

74

shadow assumes reveals one aspect of the generating figure, but not all of them taken together can show forth its *true* form because it is solid and they are plane—the derived forms are lower-dimensional with relation to the parent form, their archetype: the shadow-images are but the patterns made by a more perfect and all-inclusive form, more "real" also in the sense that it is a form less subject to mutation and change—less related to time and "seven-hued circumstance."

This is going over the same ground as before, the lighted wall taking the place of the surface of the pond, the shadows cast upon that wall, the place of the tracings made in that surface; but the idea I wish to convey seems to me important—that phenomenality and materiality, which seem to us so real and so important, may be but shadows cast on the lighted screen of sensuous existence by their higher-dimensional prototypes—the archetypal forms and beings of a higher-dimensional world.

Of the true nature of such beings, and the true forms of the forms of that higher world we can, of course, have no adequate conception, any more than it is possible to gain a true idea of a human body solely by the imprints a bather might leave in the sand. To visualize a single form which is the aggregate of an unlimited number of cross-sections, and to visualize it from their evidence alone, is difficult, indeed impossible. To escape this difficulty, instead of trying to conceive of the archetype as a form, think of it rather as a mathematical formula or process (like finding the root of a number) which, though always identical in operation, produces different results by reason of the different values given to the terms or factors; or, better still, as a unified concatenation of forces through the operation of which an infinity of forms are produced, similar in structure, but infinitely various in detail. A concrete example is the statement that every snowflake is unlike every other, though all have the familiar tetrahedral arrangement of parts and other constant characteristics. This can only mean that in the crystallization of water-vapor there is a force which always operates in a particular manner, along known mathematical lines, and however much snowflakes differ from one another, each is a dramatization in terms of form of this force and the lines along which it operates. From this it is not difficult to conceive of a generic form which is the archetype of all snowflakes. Mr. Best-Maugard, in his *A Method of Creative Design,* makes a helpful suggestion in this connection:

76

We can form our own idea of a certain archetype by studying the types which are derived from it. Suppose we wanted to form the conception of the archetypal "flower." We would analyze carefully from nature an infinite number of different kinds of flowers, and search in botany, as well as in other possible ways, for all the known and unknown laws that effect the being, purpose, function, and structure of a flower, and discover what are its essentials. The abstract idea will be a conception of the "archetype."

Plato's famous parable in his *Republic* concerning the shadow-watchers presents the idea of archetypes and the archetypal world in much the same fashion as it has been here presented, but more elaborately and dramatically. He asks the reader to imagine captives chained in a cave in such fashion that they cannot turn their heads to see a fire which burns behind them, who behold, on the illuminated wall of the cave facing them (the only thing their fetters permit them to see) the shadows of persons passing at their back, between themselves and the fire. These are talking to one another, and bearing variously shaped objects in their hands and on their heads. Seeing only these shadows and hearing voices which appear to emanate from them, these shadow-watchers cannot but believe that the shadows are

77

real and living, whereas life and reality are in the
shadow-casters, those archetypes by reason of which
alone the shadow-world exists at all. The moral of
this fable is, of course, that everything which seems
to us real—phenomenality and materiality—consists
of only the "shadows" cast by an archetypal world beyond the range of our perceptions; and it is we ourselves who occupy the position of the chained captives.

In thinking of archetypes one unconsciously reverts
to Plato. It may sound strange, and even silly, to
assert that there are archetypes of such prosaic objects as a chair, a table, or a bed, but such was clearly
his idea. Let us look into this for a moment: A chair
has, first of all, a definite function, and for every
function there should exist an appropriate form. A
chair has a direct and vital relation to the human
figure, its general size and shape being predetermined
by the size and shape of the torso and the limbs, and
by the need for resisting the pressures exerted when
the body is in a sitting position. The archetypal
chair now begins to create itself in the imagination:
we know, in a general way, what it must be like, and
although it may be subject to innumerable variations
by reason of differences of style and material, the
archetypal pattern will shine through them all, the

chair taken from the tomb of Tutankhamen being *in essence* no different from that in which I sit.

It is from the timeless archetypal world, or world of causes, that new ideas and new images emanate, together with new faculties to apprehend them, for perception itself evolves—"perception has a destiny." From that world there is at the present time a tremendous pressure upon all those who keep themselves plastic by refusing to crystallize. For in them is ʹ ʹeloping the fourth form of the manifestation of consciousness described by Ouspensky, the *intuitional*, as distinguished from the present third form, the rationalistic. The intuitives and the rationalists constitute what he calls "the two races of men," and all ethnic, religious, class, and cultural differences are unimportant in the light of the *evolutionary* difference involved in this classification. The people who constitute this minority, with their incipient fourth form of consciousness, react to everything differently from the big, bromidic mass because without themselves realizing it, they are penetrating into the archetypal world. They are, therefore, less interested in *the world-aspect*—facts and phenomena—than in *the world-order*; all unknowingly it is the archetype which has become the object of their quest.

This is amusingly indicated in their æsthetic preferences and reactions. In music they are preoccupied with tone, timbre, rhythm, subtlety, nuance, and those elements potent in arousing the primal, universal, orgiastic feelings and emotions, which cannot be done by the mere tickling of the ear with sugary tunes. In sculpture and painting they prefer generalization, indication, and suggestion to a literal and realistic rendering, because these are more emancipating to the imagination and stimulating to the imagination; as in ancient Chinese art, so definitely archetypal, they seek the significant and permanent aspect of things in contradistinction to the accidental and ephemeral. Gordon Craig, in his book, *Scene*, tells how he made hundreds of little models of man's habitations throughout the ages in his endeavor to discover, by a process of elimination, the elements common to them all, with the idea of combining these essentials into a single scene which should be *archetypal*, and where, for that reason, with the aid of light, color, and mobility, a great variety of dramatic representations could take place. Jay Hambidge's "root rectangles" of Dynamic Symmetry, and Adolfo Best-Maugard's "seven forms" are in a sense archetypal, and derive from the same archetype, the logarithmic spiral, which is perhaps the form of the universe itself—a spiral nebula. In some of the newer "stream-of-consciousness" novels "seven-hued circumstance" is made to yield a sense of that eternalness to which time is related as the falling sands are related to the hourglass.

In the field of science, the theory of relativity and the new psychology have made us acutely aware of the fact that we know only the form of our knowledge of the world which surrounds us, and not the world-in-itself. As Arthur Stanley Eddington says:

We have found a strange footprint on the shores of the unknown. We have devised profound theories to account for its origin. At last we have succeeded in reconstructing the creature that made the footprint. And lo! it is our own.

The higher-space hypothesis, with the revolutionary ideas of time and motion which it has introduced, suggests the thought that movement, growth, and becoming in the physical world are perhaps as illusory as the movement of houses, trees, telegraph poles seen from a rapidly moving railroad train: that consciousness alone moves, and that time and phenomena are the result of the movement of consciousness in a "space" which it can perceive only partially and bit by bit, and to which we can give only such a name as the fourth dimension, but which is the archetypal world in the sense in which I have tried to define it. Conceptions of this order pave the way to an idealism in no way counter to the newest science, which itself tends toward the transcendental, the mystical—a mysticism founded not upon faith, but upon knowledge.

The contradiction involved in the idea of a universe which is at the same time a multiverse, both infinite and finite, is resolved, after a fashion, in this concept of the higher-dimensional archetype and the lower-dimensional images thereof. What is God? Man's archetype. What are men? God's images— manifold, disturbed, distorted, shattered, scattered, forming, and re-forming like the reflections made by sun or moon on agitated water. Limited as we are to this plane of manifestation in which everything we see or sense, including our own personal selves, is only *reflection*, we may know that divine archetype only in the sense and to the degree that an image might conceivably know its generating object, separated from it by a dimensional chasm. And yet between the two there is a point-to-point correspondence—perfect in every detail provided that the reflecting waters are clear and still. The task which therefore confronts the aspirant to God-conscious-

82

ness is to *become* clear and still. What is the next step? Here again our analogy is a help: from every point in the image are rays which extend from object to image. But these rays are in a direction at right angles to every direction in the plane of manifestation. Therefore, to reach and become one with the object it is necessary *to transcend the plane of manifestation.* By developing the fourth form of consciousness, the intuitional, through the practice of Yoga and the intending of the mind upon the archetypal world, each may discover his particular "ray" and ascend by means of it to that world, effecting the union of the soul with the universal spirit, which is man's evolutionary goal.

I will arise and go to my father.

VII

ART AND THE MACHINE AGE

IT IS ONE OF THE FUNCTIONS OF ART "TO SHOW THE very age and body of the time his form and pressure." By this index alone it should be possible to gauge the force and fluctuations of the spiritual tide. For art is something more than the expression of man's habits, tastes, and beliefs; it is the projection also of his hopes, his aspirations, and his dreams. But living as we do in a period of scepticism and fear, there is little of this higher type of art, and perhaps our nearest approach to true æsthetic expression is in the field of invention, engineering, and manufacturing. A steel bridge, an automobile, an airplane, all products of a concerted effort toward space-conquest, their forms determined by their functions and expressive of them, come closer to being art than many of the things which go by that name, even though they do not represent the highest type of art, because "going places" ministers to no *spiritual* need.

Let us begin this survey with the World's Columbian Exposition at Chicago, in 1893, for it was there, in Machinery Hall, that the discerning mind of

One of Oskar Hansen's two winged figures at Boulder Dam, representing the spiritual and physical unity of man.

Henry Adams came to the realization that science had "electrocuted Santa Claus," and from then on the Machine would dominate men's minds and lives. But the architecture and sculpture of that Exposition gave no hint of any change: New York Central locomotive 999, flanked by two Ionic columns, confronted a Doric peristyle and a gigantic figure of Columbia clad in a Grecian robe, at the far end of a Court of Honor reminiscent only of ancient Rome and Renaissance Italy; nor was there much behind the classic façade of the Hall of Fine Arts to remind one of the Mechanical Man already knocking at its door. Only Louis Sullivan's Transportation Building, relegated to the Exposition's back yard, so to speak, sounded a note more modern and looked like what it was: a not too pretentious or permanent enclosure for the display and housing of exhibits, of an appropriately festal appearance not reminiscent of any alien or ancient grandeurs.

Sullivan was the first American Modernist, the prophet and precursor of everything sound and good done under that banner since his time. The kind of building which he so eloquently advocated and (less successfully) practised was in part realized and brought into being by reason of the World War and the subsequent Great Depression, for this re-

sulted in the usurpation in many instances of the
architect's function by the efficiency expert and the
engineer. It was the growing importance of such
functionaries in a field which had been the architect's own which converted him to his new attitude,
in which considerations of economy and efficiency
take precedence over artistic preferences. Other factors have been the example and influence of that
modern European school represented by the French
architect Le Corbusier, the credo of which is stated
in his book, Toward a New Architecture, and a de-
layed acceptance of those ideas put forward by Louis
Sullivan and by his pupil (but not his disciple),
Frank Lloyd Wright.

By reason of this change of fashion a great deal
of "applied" architecture which used to be considered necessary on purely æsthetic grounds—
cornices, columns, pilasters, pediments, which served
no useful purpose—has been done away with; and
this has been carried to such lengths that architecture appears now to have reached what might be
called the strip-tease stage, buildings have so little
"on." To realize the extent of this denuding process,
it is only necessary to compare the later with the
earlier incarnations of two famous New York institutions: the new stark and white Waldorf-Astoria

with the red and bedizened old one; and the new home of Tiffany and Company, a simple stone, steel, and glass parallelepipedon, with the earlier one, Stanford White's elaborately arched and pillared Venetian palace of the full-blown Renaissance.

The concept of a building as a working mechanism has superseded the idea of it as a work of architectural art. The beauty sought for is of a different kind: that which springs naturally from appropriateness and utility, and of such an adaptation of means to ends that any increase in fitness will be an increase also in beauty. But although the phrase, "Form Follows Function," the current architectural slogan, was Sullivan's own, he would have had scant sympathy with those practitioners who would make of architecture a purely utilitarian art, eschewing ornament on the ground that the machine, their chosen archetype, admits none. Sullivan's archetype was not the machine, but the *organism*, with that excess of beauty which is in the gay-colored convolutions of the orchid, which is in the peacock's tail and the parrot's wing. He held that ornament was an integral part of architecture. Himself one of the greatest of all creators of appropriate and original architectural ornament, he could yet write: "It would be greatly to our æsthetic good if we should refrain from the use of ornament for a period of years in order that our thought might be concentrated acutely upon the production of buildings well-formed and comely in the nude."

This is exactly what has happened, but Sullivan would not have had us be content with that. "We feel instinctively," he says, "that our strong, athletic, simple forms will carry with natural ease the raiment of which we dream; that our building, half-hid, as it were, in the products of the loom and the mine, will appeal with redoubled power." Ornament is related to structure as song is related to speech, as dancing is related to walking: it represents excess vitality—the spilled wine from a cup overfull. If to the self-styled functionalists ornament is taboo, may it not be because they have so little joy of life they do not want to dance and sing? For were that lyric spirit strong enough in them it would express itself in ornament.

But the modernistic architecture of this Machine Age—stripped, utilitarian, scornful of mere prettiness—in which the ideas of practicality and profit take precedence over æsthetic considerations of the old sort, has this great merit: it is in tune with the times, and expressive of them; it is a *face*, and not a mask, which so much of the eclectic architecture of the antecedent cycle could not but be.

The same thing is true also of the other arts in so far as they have succumbed to the spirit of the Machine Age: they are in tune with the times too, their very stridency proclaiming it. If hot numbers and hit songs, boogie-woogie and swing take precedence over Bach, Beethoven, and Brahms, it means only that the former sound the modern note and move to the current tempo, which, like the traffic, is stop-and-go. Jitterbug dancing and pivoting about a fixed point on a crowded dance floor have supplanted the old dance-forms for a similar reason: the frenetic activity of the one and the dead-alive passivity of the other correspond to some change in consciousness, which is stop-and-go too!

A significant new factor enters into these new modes which the old ones did not have: *improvisation*. This is characteristic both of swing music and of the dancing which goes with it, and it can only mean greater freedom within set forms, or the breaking down of set forms altogether. Rude and crude as this improvisation may sometimes seem— though in the hands of good performers it can be extraordinarily felicitous and artful—it hints at possible future developments in these arts not before imagined, involving the active exercise of the *intuition*, by reason of which a group is able to energize as a unit, dominated by a common consciousness. Some of the better swing bands seem able to achieve this already, with results incomparably more exciting than the old routine way of every man's eyes on his own score, intent on his part only, unconscious of his fellows, and indifferent to the music as a whole.

In modern sculpture there appears to be a return to beginnings, a seeking for the archetype: the forms of men, women, and animals resolved into their essential geometrical elements; or the exaggeration —even the distortion—of the figure in the interests of the ideal intended to be conveyed. This is in the nature of a reaction from those once so admired anatomically correct reproductions of the model, painstakingly done, as with the aid of calipers—the sort of thing which Brancusi once characterized as "cadavers." Such seem less suited to adorn the new type of light, bright, steel and glass and leather-upholstered interiors now in vogue than do the more generalized and freely-fabricated products of the sculptors' art, such as Melias Brancusi's own shining creations in which everything is subordinated to the dominant function—fishes and birds being represented as water-cleaving or air-cleaving forms. And the same thing is true of painting: no matter how much one may love and admire the old masters, or the pictorial art of yesteryear, the works of Matisse, Van Gogh, Marin, or Georgia O'Keefe (to mention four at random) in which the decorative and color-elements are more in evidence seem better in keeping with those stripped and stream-lined rooms in which the younger generation appears to find itself most at home.

It was in France, in the seventies, that artists began their first retreat from realism by painting in a manner which seemed to them more real; namely, by trying to render the effect of light on objects— what the eye saw without the corrective intervention of the mind. This went by the appropriate name of Impressionism. With every fresh retreat they dug themselves a new redoubt, hoisted a flag, and proclaimed a new *ism*: Post-impressionism, Neo-impressionism, Cubism, Futurism, Orphism, Expressionism, Dadaism, Surrealism, and what not. Soon there were so many *isms* that the artists themselves got mixed up.

New York was given its first startled glimpse of this sort of thing in the so-called Armory Show of

1913, though Alfred Stieglitz had previously exhibited some examples in "291," his devotee-haunted little studio on Fifth Avenue. The Armory showing, to the surprise of its promoters and backers, made a great stir. The works there displayed, though branded as insane, indecent, puerile, decadent, by outraged critics of the old school, aroused so much controversy and attracted such attention by reason of all this free publicity, together with clever exploitation on the part of importers and dealers, that they began to be taken seriously: the new art became fashionable, gained advocates, purchasers, and (as was bound to happen) disciples and imitators.

Perhaps never in history has so much blatant, inept, incompetent, ugly, pretentious painting been produced as by the camp-followers of that heroic handful of real artists flying the modernistic banner —heroic, because it entailed courage, devotion, sacrifice, as pioneering in any field inevitably does. These men did not form a compact and united group like the French Impressionists of an earlier day, but were separated both in time and in space, and they warred not only on established conventions, but sometimes on one another. The old art-crystal had to be broken up, "lest one good custom should corrupt the world." It was necessary to show the very age and body of the time its form and pressure, and 'if that age were decadent and its form ugly, the necessity was not less, but greater.

What all this ferment—good, bad, and indifferent —really accomplished was well stated by Gordon Craig, after seeing an exhibition in London similar to the New York Armory Show: The city, strident, ugly, vulgar, had at last invaded the Abode of Art, theretofore a sanctuary and a refuge against ugliness. No wonder there was consternation among the devotees at this profanation. The human libido, kept decorously under, had escaped from its leash, and in manifold aspects ranged free throughout the Sacred Edifice, uncontrolled and un-housebroken. What a mess! But with it all there was an outpouring of fresh vitality; here and there were glimpses of a new kind of beauty. As Whistler said: "Art happens," and perhaps it is happening now, but in so questionable a guise as to appear something other. It has made us open our eyes to new aspects of life, to other dimensions of experience. Something has started here, the value and importance of which can only be appraised as it recedes in time. The real point is that modern painting has tuned in to these times, reflects today's consciousness, has given up telling the old, agreeable lies.

No survey of art in America should omit mention of Mexico. Somewhere in the nineteen twenties José Juan Tablada, the well-known Mexican poet and novelist, and at that time the New York correspondent of *El Universal*, encouraged and assisted a number of talented young men representative of various phases of Mexican culture to come to that city. It was a happy idea, for by reason of the personal charm and brilliant talents of these unofficial ambassadors, we became Mexico-conscious as we had not been before. Miguel Covarrubias quickly became famous for his paintings, his stage-settings, and his matchless series of caricatures in *Vanity Fair*. The figurines in wax of Luis Hidalgo, exhibited, written about, illustrated, started a fashion— and so it went. Older and even more illustrious Mexican artists came to New York also, attracted by the larger opportunities it offered and perhaps by American dollars—then, as now, worth so much more than Mexican dollars. Notable among these were Adolfo Best-Maugard, Diego Rivera, and Clemente Orozco.

Following its bitter and bloody Revolution, Mexico had undergone an educational and cultural development perhaps unmatched anywhere else in the world, for it has since become historic. In the field of æsthetics Best-Maugard was a most important pioneer. For it was he who conceived the idea and designed the costumes and décor for that Aztec ballet with which the great Pavlova week after week delighted the people of the city of Mexico, and afterwards the world at large. It opened Mexican artists' eyes to their ancient heritage of beauty and removed an inferiority complex with regard to those European nations whose art they had been slavishly copying, by making them realize that they themselves had an architecture and a folk-lore as fine as any in the world.

What Ernest F. Fenollosa in an earlier cycle did for Japan, Best-Maugard did for Mexico: he turned the attention of the native artist and connoisseurs away from the then-fashionable alien art of Europe to their own art of long ago. In an exhaustive analysis of this art he discovered that it was made up of seven primary forms, each some projected fragment or aspect of a three-dimensional spiral. By visiting the museums of Europe he found that this held true of all primitive art the world over. He embodied these findings in his book, A Method of Creative Design, and with the coöperation of the then Minister of Education, this method was broadcast by a means analogous to the chain letter. That is, Best-Maugard would instruct a group of teachers, each of whom would then instruct another group, and so on until the method had been taught to more than two hundred thousand pupils. Not only did this effectively turn the tide toward the home-grown product, but it had so liberating an effect on the Mexican children trained in this method, that their work, exhibited in other countries, excited the admiration of artists all over the world. Covarrubias was one of Best-Maugard's teacher-pupils, and his work bears evidence of it, even today. A *Method of Creative Design*, published in English in 1926, had a large sale, and was adopted as a text-book in many American schools.

Rivera and Orozco, in their different ways, had been part of that vital and vitalizing stream which flowed straight from the heart of the Mexican peo-ple following their struggle against political and clerical domination. Through them this stream found outlet in an art-expression the most forceful, popular, and truly proletarian of modern times. The feeling aroused can only be compared to the parad-ing of Cimabue's painted Madonna through the streets of Florence. Rivera and Orozco used their art as a language with which to preach what they believed, and to protest the wrongs and injustices from which they felt the people suffered. Arrived in New York, they did the same thing there—or tried to: witness Orozco's grim and bitter frescoes on the walls of the New School for Social Research in New York, and Rivera's great mural for Rockefeller Center in New York, so "strong" that it had to be taken down and a composition by José Maria Sert substituted. These men are largely responsible for introducing the note of social significance ("Sing Me a Song of Social Significance") into American painting, as well as influencing its technique, as innumerable paintings and acres of murals throughout the length of the land eloquently attest.

Many of these latter paintings were commissioned by the Federal Government to keep artists from starving (though in some cases whitewash would have been better), which raises the question of the wisdom of this kind of art patronage. But in a Democracy such as ours, which by an inexorable (and let us hope beneficent) necessity assumes more and more a broad social responsibility, such a thing seems inevitable, and ought to be successful if the right people are put in control. Illustrious examples of such success are Oskar Hansen's great winged figures and astronomical pavement at

Boulder Dam, on the Arizona-Nevada boundary, Carl Milles' slowly-revolving onyx Indian, in the St. Paul City Hall, and the late Bertram Goodhue's fine capitol building at Lincoln, Nebraska, of which Lee Lawrie's sculpture forms so integral a part.

The return of sculpture and painting to their great mother, Architecture, as exemplified in the last-named building and in Radio City, Rockefeller Center, New York, and elsewhere, is a heartening sign. Hopeful also is the entrance of such able designers as Norman Bel Geddes, Walter Dorwin Teague, and (in a more restricted way) Rockwell Kent into the field of industrial designing. Not only has this brought simplicity and distinction into such things as gas ranges, refrigerators, beds, trains, automobiles, and advertising layouts and packaging, but it has made the so-called Captains of Industry realize the value of a kind of talent with which they would not now willingly dispense.

By reason of this alliance between big business and art in one of its more pedestrian aspects, there has come about a tie-up between science and art which did not formerly exist. The designer must first of all prove himself practical and economical, approaching every problem from that angle, and availing himself of every aid which science and research can offer. Indeed, the character of the new architecture has been in great part determined by the approach to the problem of shelter from the standpoint of economy and efficiency first of all. Cantilever construction, structural glass, stainless steel, and other recent products of American invention are rapidly developing new forms and combinations which will shake down into something not less definitely an architectural style than are the historic styles of the past, for the reason that these in their day were developed by an analogous process. Today the sculptor who does not seek the aid of mathematics and physics; the painter, of chemistry and spectral analysis—of everything, indeed, which on the technical side science can offer—finds himself at a disadvantage, even though in the search for transcendental beauty, which is the true aim of art, science will help him not at all—except in so far as the quest for truth, which is the true aim of science, is a search for transcendental beauty too.

The most significant signs of æsthetic newness and vitality are not to be sought today in artists' studios, or in exhibitions of pictures and statuary. What is there displayed is of small interest except to connoisseurs, artists, and to that privileged, purchasing class to which they cater, and represents only a specialized phase of American life and character. Look for that newness rather in the work of Walt Disney, in Hollywood, where the time dimension is being added to pictorial art. For in the animated picture the pictorial artist is at last able to realize his fondest dream: that of making the creatures of his imagination move and speak. This marvelous device—animation—started as a comic strip, and its use has for the most part been confined to slapstick comedy of the order of "Mickey Mouse" and "Popeye the Sailor," or fairy stories such as "Snow White," and "Pinocchio." Only in Walt Disney's latest important creation, "Fantasia," and only in certain parts of that, has this new medium revealed its latent possibilities. In the early part of "Fantasia" wherein is pictured the beginnings of sentient life on earth, from the fire-mist to the death of the dinosaurs, to the accompaniment of Stravinsky's strident music; and again in the "sound track" sequence, showing the colors and forms which the sounds of different instruments might assume, had we the eyes to see them, Disney has himself become the great emancipator from the merely foolish and the merely funny, for there is not a laugh in either of these sections, but awe and terror in the one, and

Sculptural detail by Lee Lawrie, from the State Capitol building at Lincoln, Nebraska.

an entirely new kind of beauty in the other. Here are intimations of a new art form, compounded of sound, form, color, and mobility—color-music, in point of fact.

Though totally different in character, size, material, and setting, the nightly fountain display at the New York World's Fair in the summers of 1939 and 1940 induced somewhat similar psychological reactions in the beholder. This was because that display was compounded of much the same elements as was "Fantasia," namely: moving masses, changing forms, effects of light and color, the whole synchronized to amplified orchestral music. Hailed as the finest, as well as the most popular feature of the Fair, it, almost alone, justifies the title of "The World of Tomorrow," for here indeed one got a glimpse of a possible art-development unlike anything which the past can offer, powerful and beautiful, worthy, in my opinion, to rank with the Pyramids and the Parthenon. Since art comes from excess of life, its beginnings should be looked for where the human tide flows strongest. The Court of Fountains, on Flushing Meadows, was surely one of such places, and the Great White Ways of the twelve cities in which "Fantasia" was nightly shown are some of the many others.

The Machine Age represents a period of power—
if only for destruction. When power attains a certain maximum it not infrequently changes to beauty
—after the stalk, the flower; after the Iron Age, the
Golden. But this Golden Age can come only as the
result of some fresh outpouring of spiritual life,
some change in the universal consciousness. Signs
are not lacking that such a change is even now imminent. Today the ideals of human liberty and human brotherhood move millions to those ardors and
renunciations which have marked the religious manifestations of times past. When these ideals are at
last triumphant, mankind will weave marvelous patterns on the space-time loom unlike any ever made
before, and inferior to none. Art in the Machine
Age, however poor in its performance, still holds
this promise.

VIII

SKYSCRAPERS

OF ALL OUR ARCHITECTURAL FLORA THE SKYSCRAPER alone is truly native: our churches, courthouses, libraries, museums, banks are for the most part uninspired adaptations of stale European originals, but the skyscraper is all our own, an expression and a symbol of the American spirit—that ruthless, tireless, assured *energeticism* delightedly proclaiming, "What a great boy am I!"

It is popularly supposed that the skyscraper arose as a result of the impossibility of lateral expansion, lower Manhattan with its confining rivers, and the Chicago Loop—the districts wherein these buildings first shot skyward—being cited in proof of this. But the Loop is not a nature-made but a man-made barrier—metaphysical, not physical—while an aerial view of New York reveals vast tracts of low-lying buildings between the Wall Street district and its encircling rivers.

No, the origin of the skyscraper was psychological: it arose in answer to the desire of the herd to become a super-herd—of spot-cards to become face-cards. Skyscrapers appear only and always on these sacred acres which for some reason have become the blue heaven of the business man. High buildings in preferred areas owe their existence to the same cause as high prices for front-row seats at a show—the desire to be an insider, for the high places at the feast.

But from another point of view the skyscraper came into being as the result of an effort to get the better of the real-estate agent and the tax collector by expanding in the free dimension, capturing and turning to profit more than an equitable share of the common air and sunlight. Ugly as the word may sound, the skyscraper is a product of human greed, thus standing in symbolic relation to the times. I hasten to add, however, that this motive is less ignoble than those which have inspired some of the noblest buildings in the world, for was not the Colosseum built for spectacles of sanguinary slaughter? The sordidness of the motive is lost sight of in the greatness of the achievement, just as the hook and bait which landed him are swallowed up in Leviathan. This is all part of that paradox so disconcerting to our moralities: the favorite food of epicures springs from the dung-heap, and from ground richly manured by dollars spring sky-piercing Valhallas, crowned with light. It militates not at all against the skyscraper that in the last analysis it is a product of greed, and an enclosure for the transaction of sharp bargains, so long as we do not call it a Cathedral of Commerce, and try to make it look like something other than it is. Hypocrisy in architecture is as ugly as it is in life, while simple honesty somehow satisfies and gives forth overtones of beauty.

Of the physical factors which have gone to the shaping of the skyscraper the first, and of the first importance, is steel-frame construction—that system of riveted-together vertical and horizontal members, insuring strength, rigidity, stability—a skyscraper being a truss placed upright. Coequal with this, in the sense that vertical building would have been impossible without it, is the fast, safe passenger elevator—the very piston of the machine. And the bringing of this to its present state of perfection involved mechanical difficulties far greater than the mere piling of story upon story, once the trick was learned. Mention must also be made of the ingenious methods now in use for the sinking of foundations to great depths, for without this Chicago could never have stretched its neck as high as New York, the early Chicago skyscrapers having been floated on rafts, on a lake of mud, sometimes with perilous results. And finally, the draining, heating, lighting, water-, fire-, and wind-proofing of these buildings had all to be taken care of in order to make them possible. The inventive and mechanical ability involved in the production of a modern American skyscraper is perhaps greater than in any other thing, unless it be an ocean liner.

The skyscraper has been shaped by practical, not by æsthetic necessity. Like a bridge, though in a lesser degree, it is an engineering problem. The engineer has performed his part magnificently, because the American engineers are the most daring and competent in the world—they have to be, by reason of the demands made upon them. But the architect, glamoured by Europe and by the grandeurs of Greece and Rome, for a long time misconceived his problem, which was not to adorn the necessitous engineering structure of the skyscraper, translating it into this or that dead architectural language, but to dramatize it. Louis Sullivan was the first architect to face the problem from this viewpoint. He demonstrated by eloquent precept and a few admirable examples that a steel framework, encased within a protective fire-resisting envelope need not and should not be made to look as though the walls were of solid masonry, supporting the weight of the floors as well as their own weight, and because they support neither, he treated the walls frankly as a veneer.

Furthermore, he made the tall building "a proud and soaring thing, without a dissenting line from bottom to top," thus putting an end to the practice, common up to the time of his innovation, of piling the classic orders on top of one another, like a house of cards. Engulfed though Sullivan was in the great bromidic tide, he was an inspiration to certain young men, myself among them. As Charles Whitaker says: "He was a flash of beauty in the dull and deadly world of the American draughting room of his day, where copyists slaved over plates and photographs under the delusion that they were practicing the art of building."

Cass Gilbert, an architect of great ability (he designed the George Washington Bridge over the Hudson River), but not so bold and deep a thinker as Sullivan, conceived of the skyscraper as a "Cathedral of Commerce." The Woolworth Building, and the New York Life Building are embodiments of his idea. He argued, probably, as follows: today we make a religion of business; therefore why not treat the office building as the sacred edifice, lavishing on it all of our best? The Gothic style lends itself admirably to modern uses, for it is pre-eminently vertical, the very thing called for in a skyscraper; moreover, it is infinitely flexible, being unencumbered by

canons of proportion as the classic orders are. The
Woolworth Tower, which struck this new keynote,
is certainly "in every inch a proud and soaring
thing," and remains today in many respects the
finest of all skyscrapers. It so stimulated other architects to emulation and to imitation that Gilbert's
must be reckoned as the next most important influence after Sullivan's on skyscraper design. His
reasoning was based on false premises so far as the
use of Gothic forms and ornamentation is concerned. We can no longer think in terms of medie-
valism; therefore, logic compels us either to use no
ornament at all or else ornament of a kind consistent
with our own particular psychology. To fill Gothic
niches with effigies of noted scientists and captains
of industry instead of with saints and disciples, and
to substitute dollar signs for symbols of the Trinity
is a ridiculously wrong answer to the problem. Not
that Gilbert was ever guilty of just that, but other
architects have been. A new ornamental mode is a
thing of slow growth, and in the meantime what is
the poor architect to do? The only answer appears
to be: string your own bead necklace, however
crude, or else go bare.

The next important influence on skyscraper design after Gilbert's came in a strange way and from a

strange source: "The Loser Wins" might be the title of its story. *The Chicago Tribune* Building, widely advertised as the most beautiful skyscraper in the world, was built according to the design submitted by John Mead Howells and Raymond Hood in a world-wide competition of which they were the winners. It is in a pseudo-Gothic style, a fine piece of stage scenery made to look as picturesquely medieval as possible, the crowning lantern flanked by flying buttresses which cast interesting shadows but do not buttress, being more like hands pressed to a bewildered head engaged in thinking: "So this is Chicago! How did I get here, I wonder?"

The second prize design by Eliel Saarinen, a Finnish architect, who built the railway station at Helsingfors, was as different as could be from that of his successful rivals: simple, direct, unpretentious, with a square tower which just *stopped*, but with an indefinable felicity, by reason of subtle diminishments and other artifices. Sullivan hailed this design as a return to and a carrying forward of those principles of which he had been the advocate and exemplar. Bertram Goodhue, himself a competitor, declared that Saarinen's design was in a class by itself and superior to all the others, and such was the general opinion, both professional and lay. Observe

the workings of poetic justice: though the victory
was theirs, and the spoils of victory in good American dollars, the victors themselves were convicted of
sin and suffered conversion. For what other infer-
ence can be drawn from the New York *Daily News*
Building (on East Forty-second Street) of which
Raymond Hood was the architect, which is entirely
in the spirit of Saarinen's unsuccessful design for
The Chicago Tribune Building, and as unlike the
successful one as can well be imagined. Destitute of
any ornament except about the entrance, and of any
architectural grace save its soaring verticals and the
finely disposed, proportionately related parts, the
building somehow succeeds in making its neighbors,
the Chrysler and the Chanin buildings, look a little
bit silly by comparison. It does not seem to stand
on tiptoe blowing a silver trumpet, as does the one,
nor to give a false effect of massiveness by means of
squat pilasters and artificial buttresses as does the
other, but it assumes to be only what it is: a work of
structural engineering, a cliff-like human hive, a
monster of the mere market. Saarinen's influence on
skyscraper architecture has been pronounced, particularly in Chicago, where his formula has been followed in the Board of Trade and in the Palmolive
buildings; but these merely brought to a focus cer-

tain tendencies which had already been making themselves felt and which reached their full flowering in the Rockefeller Center group—simple rectilinear masses, soaring lines, no crowning cornices, and a general absence of applied ornament.

The final influence to be noted is that of Hugh Ferris, who is not in the strict sense an architect at all but an architectural "renderer." His architectural sense and his æsthetic sensitiveness are, however, so superior to those of most of the architects who employ him to make pictures of their buildings that it is often highly disillusioning to compare his drawings with their originals. Ferris served his masters so well that he enslaved some of them. His book, *The Metropolis of Tomorrow*, appears to have exerted an influence on skyscraper design analogous to that which Piranesi's prison etchings exercised on George Dance's design for Old Newgate. Turning the pages of Ferris's book, we may read not only the last skyscraping word, but the one which has not yet been uttered. Both Hugh Ferris and Frank Lloyd Wright have conceived of the skyscraper of the future as having walls of metal and glass, *hung* like clothes on a line, from the steel framework. Such a next step would be entirely consistent and logical: a building all of shining metal and glass would constitute a more honest and eloquent dramatization of the essentials of a skyscraper than those now current, because it is not, in essence, a masonry structure, though made to appear as though it were. The lofty rectilinear steel frames of skyscrapers outlined in black and orange against the blue of the sky, have always been to me a marvel and a delight, but no sooner have they been encased in masonry than the chief element of their charm has vanished—that *strong lightness*. For they are so strong that their structural limit of height far overpasses the economic limit, and they are so light that the finished edifice weighs less than the rock removed to give foothold and cellarage.

Having traced the evolution of the skyscraper even beyond the point at which it stands today, I might here make an end, but this survey would be superficial did I not now continue in a somewhat different strain.

An incorrigible symbolist, I cannot but attach symbolical significance to the fact that one may turn page after page of *The Metropolis of Tomorrow* without coming upon a single human figure: here is pictured a world from which humanity appears to have perished, done to death by the realization of its

own egregious dream. The skyscraper is fundamentally inhuman, not because its construction
exacts the toll of a workman killed for every story
erected, but because it has arisen in defiance of the
common rights of common humanity, and this will
probably in the end achieve its doom. For if tall
buildings continue to multiply, traffic congestion—
for which they are directly responsible—will become
traffic paralysis, and conditions will be created not
unlike those pictured in the cinema *Metropolis*,
wherein everyone lives and works, in effect, under-
ground, except the overlords, who have pre-empted
the right to breathe the free air and look upon the
sky. The skyscraper's advantage is gained at the ex-
pense of its more lowly neighbor, but when the
owners of the surrounding property avail themselves
of their own inalienable right to build skyscrapers,
no one benefits. Unnatural and intolerable conditions are the inevitable results.

But under more drastic restrictions which might
conceivably be imposed, the advantages of this manner of vertical expansion would be too many and
too great to be foregone. Such advantages could be
insured only under conditions long familiar to every
student of the science of cities, but impossible of
fulfillment now, short of a social revolution and a

change of consciousness on the part of almost everyone concerned. As Le Corbusier, Ferris, and other city planners have made plain, skyscrapers should be erected only at focal points where traffic lanes converge, and the surrounding buildings should be kept relatively low and sufficiently distant, as they are in Rockefeller Center; or else broad avenues, flanked by high buildings, should alternate with narrower streets, flanked by low ones. It is obvious, however, that under the existing governmental and social regime, property laws, and system of land-ownership, such solutions will continue to remain only a city-planner's dream.

A city ought to be a garden and not a jungle. One night as I sat on the roof of the Hotel Shelton, watching a fish-shaped blimp swimming about in the blue void above me, I was momentarily subject to the illusion that all the buildings were a weedy growth at the bottom of some gigantic aquarium, so unrelated to reason and order did they seem.

But putting aside all sociological, moralistic, and narrowly æsthetic considerations, if we look at these megatheria of commerce with something of the detachment and young-eyed wonder which we are able to bring to the contemplation of the Pyramids—to which they are related as life to death—we shall see

114

these buildings most truly. So great is our immersion, however, in the dense medium which produced them, that this is more difficult for us than for the foreigner visiting our shores. A world-battered, hard-boiled Englishman confessed to me that his first vision of the towers of Manhattan, sun-illumined above the low-lying Atlantic mist, moved him to tears for some reason which he could not understand; and a cynical but sensitive Frenchman, on beholding the same sight on another occasion, was heard to murmur: *"C'est beau, c'est grand, c'est vrai!"*

Such emotion, such enthusiasm, does them honor, and is a far finer thing than our own unimaginative acceptance of what is surely the eighth wonder of the world. Silhouetted against the gray of dawn, the crimson of sunset, or bright with the radiance of mid-day; rain-drenched, mist-enveloped, or piercing the darkness with late-lighted windows and shining coronets of flame, these campanili of the New Feudalism—however base-born and æsthetically uninspired, are none the less the planet's most august and significant symbol of proud-spirited man "flashing unquenched defiance to the stars."

IX

HARNESSING THE RAINBOW

IN AN ANTECEDENT LECTURE I PREDICTED THAT THE new art-form of the coming age would be color music. Such an art is now for the first time possible by reason of the high development of illuminating engineering, but before it can happen, light must be rescued by the creative artist from the engineers and the advertisers who have put this "divine covenant" to ignoble uses. Some results of their collaboration may be viewed nightly in Times Square in New York, and in the Great White Ways of other cities. These displays, with all their lack of artistry, yield sometimes effects of amazing beauty. This is owing to the inherent nature of light itself: *it cannot be vulgarized.*

A more potent medium than sound, which is of the earth sphere, light links us to the farthest visible star. Moreover, the field of vision is immensely richer and more various than that which is apprehensible by the ear. When I told Leopold Stokowsky that I was working on a color-organ, his comment was that color music should be more marvelous than his kind

Thomas Wilfred at the keyboard of his Clavilux, or mobile color instrument.

One of the "solo figures" projected by the Clavilux.

of music, because light is so much more wonderful a thing than sound.

The difficulty consists in the inferior impressionability of the eye compared with the ear. To the average person color—as color—has nothing significant to say: he considers it always in relation to other things, not as a *thing-in-itself*. To him, grass is green, snow is white, the sky blue. To have his attention called to the fact that grass is sometimes brown or yellow; snow, blue; and the sky, green, is disconcerting. Only when his retina is assailed by some sky-encircling rainbow, aurora borealis, or splendid sunset is he able to enjoy color as color. This is because the sense of sight has never been *educated*, as hearing has been educated; for music, the dominant art for the past three hundred years, has developed the ear into so fine an instrument that it can distinguish harmonics and resolve a chord into its component notes, whereas the education of the eye to nuances of color is only just beginning. My experience in the theater convinced me that few people think about or really see light, though everyone is affected by it. Comedy scenes cannot be played in a cold or dim light because such light is unconsciously depressive, whereas a warm, bright light induces the mood for laughter. Red light is exciting, blue light, sedative. These are truisms of the theater, based on experience. The popular response to the fountain display at the New York World's Fair, which was a phase of the very thing I am speaking about—color-music, the elements of which are sound, form, color, and mobility organized into a language of emotional expression—is an indication that the education of the eye has indeed begun. This fountain display was the creation of Bassett Jones, a man who learned about light and color in the only school in which it can be learned—the theater. He used to do all the lighting for Maude Adams' productions, and is the inventor of theatrical lighting equipment not yet outmoded.

Let me briefly sketch the history of color-music. The conception, like that of flying in the air, is an old one: If the visible spectrum were divided into twelve parts it would yield a color-scale corresponding to the musical chromatic scale of twelve semitones. Any piece of music could then be translated into its color equivalent, and there you are! It was on this basis that the first mobile color instruments were constructed—Bainbridge Bishop's, A. P. Rimington's, and my own first machine—the "Luxorgan." But it was the wrong idea, as I shall later endeavor to make plain. Bishop's color organ was just an ordinary reed organ upon which was superimposed a framed semi-circular sheet of ground glass upon which appeared a play of colored light controlled by the organ keyboard, and based upon the "musical parallel" above referred to. Coming before the electric light, daylight was admitted from behind, and this was modified by shutters of variously colored glass. Rimington's instrument was along similar lines, both being played from a musical score upon an organ keyboard, but Rimington, having the advantage of electric light, projected his color-music upon a distant screen, stereopticon-wise. At a laboratory on Long Island of which I was the architect— the first of its kind, so far as I know—Thomas Wilfred developed and built his Clavilux, first shown at the Neighborhood Playhouse, New York. It was better than any instrument of a corresponding nature, made either before or since. Wilfred disregarded the musical parallel altogether, as I did in my later experiments. Van Deering Perrine, the painter, in the three machines which he has constructed, never bothered his head about the musical parallel at all.

I shall not tell about my experiments in this field, for they have all been failures. Certain conclusions based upon these failures are important, however.

One was that this new art-form must progress from its own beginnings and unfold in its own unique and characteristic way without reference to its sister art of music. Correspondences between the arts—such, for example, as inspired the saying that architecture is frozen music—are due to that underlying unity upon which our various modes of sense-perception act as a refracting medium, and must, therefore, be taken for granted. Each art, like each individual, is unique and singular, and in this singularity dwells its most thrilling appeal. I concluded that we shall miss the rainbow's uttermost secret and light's crowning glory if we preoccupy ourselves too much with the similarities existing between music and color, sound and light. It is rather their points of difference which should be discovered and taken advantage of.

Consider the difference between the two sense-categories to which music and color respectively appeal—hearing and seeing. This resolves itself into a comparison between time and space, because music unfolds in time, and architecture occupies space. The characteristic thing about time is succession, one thing following another, and music is perpetual change, a constant becoming. The characteristic of space, on the other hand, is simultaneousness—in space alone perpetual immobility would reign. Light and color are essentially of space, and partake of the nature of space; they should not be without a certain serenity and repose: a "tune," if it be sufficiently lively, played on a color-organ is only distressing. If there be a workable correspondence between the musical art and an art of mobile color, it will be found rather in the domain of harmony, which involves the idea of simultaneity, rather than in melody, which is pure succession. This fundamental difference between time and space as it bears on this subject cannot be overemphasized. A musical note prolonged, becomes at last scarcely tolerable; but a beautiful color, like the blue of the sky, we can enjoy all day and every day. The changing hues of a sunset are *andante* if referred to a musical standard, but to the eye they are *allegro*—we would have them pass less swiftly than they do. The winking, chasing, changing lights of illuminated sky-signs are annoying for the same reason. The eye longs for repose in some serene radiance or stately sequence, while the ear delights in contrast and continual change. It may be that as the eye becomes more educated it will welcome more movement and complexity, but a certain stillness and serenity are of the very essence of light, as movement and passion are of the nature of sound. Music is a seeking—"love in search of a word"; light is a finding—"a divine covenant."

Even assuming that a color scale can be established (as has been done) which would yield a color correlative to any musical note or chord, there remains the matter of *values* to be dealt with. In the musical scale there is a practical equality of values—each note has a positive value of its own, though all are different; one is as potent as another. In a color scale, on the other hand, the values vary widely: the blues are feeble and the yellows and reds powerful. These values have no musical correlatives, they belong to color *per se*, and as the whole secret of beauty and brilliance dwells in a proper understanding and adjustment of values, the musical parallel is of no assistance here.

It would seem that the best approach to an art of color-music would be through an examination into such emotional reactions as color can be discovered to yield. The musical art began in the emotional response to certain tones and combinations of tones, and the delight of the ear in their repetition and variation. Because of the undeveloped sensitivity of the eye to color before referred to, the emotional reactions to different colors are discovered to be largely personal and whimsical: one person "loves" pink, another, purple, or green. Color therapeutics is too new a thing to be relied on for data, for even though colors are susceptible of classification as sedative, recuperative, stimulating, or depressive, no two classifications arrived at independently would be apt to coincide. Most people appear to like bright, pure colors, when presented to them in small areas, red and blue being the favorites. Data have been accumulated regarding the physiological effects and psychological responses to different colors, but this order of research is in its infancy, and so in my later experiments in color music I had recourse to a theory, in the absence of any safer guide.

This theory is based upon the idea of man as a triplicity: a sensuous, emotional, and thinking being, this triune nature being related to the unifying and overshadowing spirit as the colors of the spectrum are related to the white light of the sun, as the notes of the musical scale are related to what the Chinese call the Great Tone.

This is in accord with that theosophic scheme derived from the Ancient Wisdom which longer than any other has withstood the obliterating action of time, and is now renascent. Let us, therefore, attempt to classify the colors of the spectrum according to this theory and discover, if we can, how nearly such a classification is conformable to reason and experience.

The red end of the spectrum, being lowest in vibratory rate, would correspond to the physical nature, proverbially more sluggish than the emotional and mental. The phrase, "like a red rag to a bull," suggests a relation between the color red and the animal consciousness, established by observation. The low-brow is the dear lover of the red necktie; the high-brow is he who sees violet shadows on the snow. We "see red" when dominated by ignoble passion. Though the color green is associated with the idea of jealousy, it is the color of sympathy, for in the last analysis jealousy is the fear of the loss of sympathy; green belongs, in any case, to the mediant, or emotional group of colors; while blue and violet are proverbially intellectual and spiritual colors, and their position in the spectrum therefore conforms to the demands of our theoretical division.

Here, then, is something certainly reasonable, reasonably certain, to be confirmed or confuted by experiment and research. Conceive, therefore, of the spectrum as divided into three groups of colors, corresponding to the true primaries, red, green, and blue, the first related to the physical, the second to the emotional, and the third to the intellectual and spiritual natures. The first group would comprise red, orange, and yellow, occupying what is called the thermal end of the spectrum, and lowest in vibratory rate. The intermediate group would be yellow-green, green, and green-blue; while the third group would comprise the colors occupying the electrical end of the spectrum and highest in vibratory rate: blue, "indigo," and violet. The colors of each group affect consciousness in a different manner, those of the first being in general stimulating, of the second tranquilizing, and of the third, subduing.

So if we are to have color symphonies, they are not likely to be based on any translation of some musical masterpiece into its color correlative according to this or that "musical parallel," but rather they will be the creations of persons who are emotionally sensitive to light and color, able to imagine in terms of it, and to treat it imaginatively.

Color-music is a thing of infinite possibilities. Into the matter of means and methods I do not propose to enter here, nor attempt to answer such questions as to whether the light should be direct or projected, whether the spectator, wrapped in darkness, should watch the music unfold at the end of some mysterious vista, or whether he should be played upon and bathed in waves of brilliant and multicolored light. Ideas multiply in bewildering profusion: sunsets, solar coronas, auroras such as were never seen on sea or land; rainbows, bubbles, rippling water; flaming volcanoes, lava streams of living light—these and myriads of other enthralling and perfectly realizable effects suggest themselves. What Israfel of the future will pour on mortals this new "music of the spheres"?

For over and above the purely æsthetic pleasure to be derived from it, color-music would undoubtedly possess therapeutic value—the beneficial effects of certain color-vibrations in the treatment of disease are already known. But the highest use and supreme function of an art of light would be the quickening of human evolution and the expansion of consciousness. Even discussing it thus is vaguely stimulating and exciting. It is as though we stood already on the confines of some brave new world.

X

THE THEATER

WHAT, IN THE LAST ANALYSIS, IS THE PLACE AND function of the theater? Immersed as we are in the immediate business of living—and of making a living —we need something which will give us a vision of life strained of its pettiness, its confusion, its discreteness, as seen from a height instead of too near at hand, thus revealing something of its pattern and its plan. For this the theater is an ideal agent; quite aside from the drama's content, by reason of the dramatic form itself, involving as it does the elimination of inessentials and the telescoping of time, we are enabled to trace the figures in life's carpet as we could not trace them without this artificial aid. For almost any slice of life, even the most insignificant or sordid, when fixed, focused, illuminated, and looked at through the aperture of a proscenium arch as under a microscope, reveals something of life's organic structure apt to pass unnoted if not thus mounted and magnified. Surely the theater can not die unless civilization itself perish.

I once saw a play on Broadway called *The Fabulous Invalid*. The title was intended to characterize the theater, which seems about to pass away, yet never does so, however menaced by the automobile, the moving pictures, the radio, and what not. The play portrayed the rise, decline, and last-minute rescue of a New York playhouse of the past century. Beginning as a resort of the highest fashion, it was gradually changed and cheapened with the changing times, becoming in turn a home for melodrama, movies, and finally burlesque so dirty that the place was raided by the police and closed. Into its darkened interior then entered an eager company of young people who needed only a theater—any theater —to realize their fondest dreams. So the entire cycle started anew. All during the progress of the drama the playhouse had been haunted by the shades of two actors, a man and a woman, who had died together on the opening night; given the choice of going to heaven or of remaining in the theater, they chose this last. Fearful of the theater's end and their consequent exile into heaven, they were joined by Shakespeare's ghost, who reassures them by telling of the vicissitudes the theater underwent in his day. "Why, when I put on *Hamlet*," he said, "the critics didn't give it a week to live, but now after more than three hundred years, it's still alive on Broadway."

The amazing vitality of this "fabulous invalid,"

the theater, is accounted for in the following manner in a Hindu folk-tale told me by my friend Dhan Gopal Mukerji, himself a dramatist: Anciently in India—so goes the story—there existed a ripe civilization which, having passed through all the phases which Western civilization has passed through, had reached that last stage when, the world's slow stain having obscured the divine image in the heart of man, his whole nature suffered corruption. Religion languished, the temples were deserted, the fires were unkindled on the altars, and the shrines were dark. A few faithful devotees prayed for the restoration of the ancient worship that the path of release from the round of births and deaths might be kept open; and Brahma, giving heed to these petitioners, after meditating profoundly, answered them thus:

"In man's progression toward the awareness of me in himself he must from time to time forsake my temples and forswear my worship, for freedom is his, being mine—I being he. But that the sacred thread may not at any time be broken, I ordain this new thing, The Theater, which, because it is my cosmic play become microcosmic, he cannot even wish to evade or escape. So, though my temples, being temporal, fall into ruin, and my worship and service be forgotten, because those who beget, forget; yet will my ritual, taking the form of dramatic representation, be never intermitted; and from his own play, man will still be able to discover his true nature and his oneness with me."

Today the tide of life flows less strong through the churches than through the Great White Ways of the world where is the theater. This would, therefore, appear to be one of those periods wherein the theater needs must perform the office of the temple or the church. As at present organized and administered, however, the theater can do this only here and there and now and then. In our great centers of population it is "a real estate proposition"—a going concern for revenue only, which offers, like the modern department store, a great variety of wares. It is, among other things, a pornographic peep-show, a comic strip, a chamber of horrors, a mental anodyne, an emotional prophylactic; and if the theater be defined as the home of the drama, in many of our playhouses the "Standing Room Only" sign should be replaced by one bearing the legend, "Nobody Home."

But in spite of all its perversions, trivialities, and abominations of one sort or another, the theater is today endowed with so lusty a life, is so manured by dollars, fed by the sap of youth, sustained by its ardors, and renewed by such willing service and glad

130

sacrifice that it has somehow managed to escape that blight of *standardization* which appears to have overcome those other potential agents of education and inspiration, the press, the radio, and the cinema (as represented by Hollywood). The theater still gives forth human sounds instead of the mere rattle of machinery, and what happens in it remains unpredictable, abounding in reversals and surprises. It is at this door—the stage door—that the youth of today are pressing with such vehemence as to constitute a sign of the times too important to be overlooked.

Fathers complain that the boy will not go into the office or the factory; mothers, that the girl will not stay in the home; ministers, that young people will not go to church and Sunday-school; teachers, that study is looked upon by the pupils as the price to be paid for participation in the school's social life. But from theatrical managers, agents, and producers one hears an altogether different story: they have to protect themselves against the hordes of young men and (particularly) maidens seeking sanctuary in the theater from office, factory, home, church, school. The theater has assumed the role of Pied Piper, whose music lures even to the perilous river's brink. This is the more significant because the commercial theater has use for only a relatively few of these young people, nor—with rare exceptions—can they gain there what they seek. In schools and colleges there is the same strange ferment: dramatics, a recent survey shows, is second only to athletics in popularity, and the increase in the number and importance of Little Theater groups throughout the country is phenomenal.

May it not be that the more sensitive and adventurous of the younger generation—those who most truly represent it—are in revolt against the cultural and educative agencies provided by their elders because these are alien to the spirit of the new age and ill-adjusted to its changed psychology; and that the reason why young people are turning toward the theater in such numbers is that they dimly feel that *it* may meet their developmental and disciplinary needs?

No, someone is sure to answer, it is because they are slack and pleasure-loving, and they want to escape discipline. Doubtless this is true in certain cases, but by whatever motives they seem—even to themselves —to be actuated, subjectively they are seeking something which their ordinary life and schooling has failed to provide, and however preposterous this may sound to the imperfectly instructed, the theater, rightly organized and administered, is indeed

A Theater and Temple of the Dance, designed by
Claude Bragdon for Ruth St. Denis and Ted Shawn.

capable of fulfilling their disciplinary, educational, and cultural needs.

The necessity for a more highly organized coöperative and communal life, which the passing generation is coming to recognize through social and economic pressure, the elect of the younger generation know intuitively, and so they try to organize their social life in their own ways—often grotesque ways—rejecting the advice, instruction, and modes of activity and entertainment proffered them by their elders, to the latter's bewilderment and chagrin. But theirs was the initial error; each generation has its own useful and necessary function with respect to the younger, but the one thing it is always trying to do is to cast youth in the same mould in which itself was cast. The world is full of loving and well-meaning parents who will do anything for their children but get off their backs.

Individual, non-competitive self-expression, together with group-consciousness and coöperation—until by some means these things are integrated into our educational system, it will fail to meet the needs of modern youth. To suggest that the theater might provide these means is my point and purpose, for the theater in its wider, deeper, nobler aspects is an unprepared though natural channel leading to these

133

very ends. Nothing, potentially at least, embraces a wider segment of life: it is a microcosm in which many different things are capable of being harmonized into a greater whole—science, history, archeology, poetry, all of the major arts and many of the minor crafts. Organized along educative lines, the theater could be made to meet the needs of developing young people as nothing else does or can do; for it would minister to the sense of beauty, arouse the imaginative and creative faculties, make of the body a fine instrument, discipline the emotions and strengthen the will. And along with this individual development it would relate the individual to the group through the primal necessity for coöperation, because nothing can be done successfully in the theater without community of effort—coöperation is of its very essence, being involved in the mere matter of making a "cross" or the giving or the receiving of a cue.

But the greatest thing of all in favor of the theater as an educative agent is the interest which it arouses, the enthusiasm which it generates. To persons who have experienced the strange, subjective, felicitous excitement which attends working intensively and creatively with others toward a common end, the fascination of the theater will be understood. In try-

ing to account for this, Mr. William M. Houghton
has this to say:

No one who has shared the real intimacy of strenu-
ous coöperation over a period of time with a congenial
group of his fellow-beings but looks back on the experience with romantic recollection. The romance is
heightened for him if there were discouraging obstacles
to be overcome by the common effort, and hard luck
and troubles in the common lot. After such an experience the ordinary world in which each of us goes
his own gait more or less seems a little cold and cheer-
less and uninteresting, and one becomes lonely for that
more intensive comradeship that one has idealized in
memory.

Now education, to be effective, cannot run counter to the deep desires of those being educated. The
theater fulfills this condition of being attractive to
youth, but to the mind of one to whom the idea of its
educative value is new and repellent, just by reason
of its unfamiliarity, the following questions naturally suggest themselves: Shall Melpomene dethrone
Athena? Shall Harlequin's cloak and mask replace
the cap and gown, and the professors become mere
masters of revels? What then becomes of the austere
ardors of scholarship, and that disciplining of the

mind rightly regarded as part of the educational ideal?

My answer is that the theater is both austere and disciplinary, with the advantage that its rigors are willingly—even joyfully incurred. There is no limit to the amount of drill, and what in other connections would be called drudgery, which young people are willing to undergo in order to achieve the things which they themselves really want to achieve, be it dancing the rhumba, playing the saxophone, or acting *Hamlet*—all of which are arduous unless undertaken for the fun of the thing. So long as their ambition and interest are engaged, young people do not falter in the face of difficulty; it is the initial lack of heat, or the subsequent lowering of temperature which is responsible for that failure of attention, that lassitude or loss of confidence which are the forerunners of defeat and the fertile cause of scholastic failure. In the theater, more readily than in the lecture room, the laboratory, or the class-room, the interest can be kept at the boiling point, because the pupil looks on the matter not as a grind, but as a game. And it is this *play spirit* which should be fostered, organized, given the right kind of an objective, and inspired to higher and higher flights.

This has been done in a small, but effective way

in the school of Edith King and Dorothy Coit in New York, apostates both from the educational orthodoxies of their day. All of the educative activities derive from, and are centered about the preparation and presentation of some play, for which the pupils design and make the costumes, scenery, and properties. They study the history, literature, and art of the country and people with which the play has to do, and receive training in music, movement, and diction. The entire curriculum pyramids up to that yearly event, the production of the play, which is in the nature of a happy apotheosis for the children, as well as a source of unique pleasure to those permitted to attend. This is only a small school for quite young children, but it is founded on an idea which has proved its worth, and is capable of almost infinite expansion.

There are doubtless many other instances of the utilization, for educational purposes, of young people's interest in, and natural aptitude for the theater; but it is safe to assume that none of them has developed all of the possibilities inherent in the idea, for the reason that these possibilities are so many and lead so far. As regards the great American universities, with only a few exceptions, the undergraduate may be said to have brought the theater to the college rather than the other way around. It has grown up like a weed in the college yard, instead of being a conservatory product. Sometimes, on its official side, the university ignores the theater; in others, patronizes it, but when parented by alma mater it is apt to lead a rather starved existence, not having been made, in any true sense, an integral part of the scholastic life.

The building, organization, administration, and endowment of theaters, their development to serve educative as well as recreational ends, should engage the serious attention of those who have the training of the youth of today in hand. The money changers have trafficked too long in this particular temple; it has been given over to base uses, and puritanism has branded it too long with its taboo. The important and honorable place which the theater has held in the history of culture should not be forgotten. In the Temple of the Future, not built with hands, this stone, which our puritanical forefathers and their prototypes of the present day have rejected, may form the very headstone of the corner.

All of which brings me back, by a long detour, to my original contention: that the theater, by virtue of some inner necessity, is indeed itself a temple; that in it the bright cloak of Harlequin, the yellow robe of Buddha, and Christ's seamless dress have become one garment, flung wide enough to cover all humanity. For the drama has an esotericism of its own (whether introduced consciously or unconsciously does not matter), and every play can have within it some mystery enfolded, like honey in a flower—food for the soul.

But the theater is a temple in another sense, and for a different reason. During those periods when religion was a living force in human life, the arts— and also many of the industries—were gathered, housed, and nourished in and about the sacred edifice which thereby became their "procreant cradle." Today it is not the church but the theater which performs this office—music, eloquence, rhythmic movement, decoration, architecture, painting, sculpture, each having at least potentially its place. These only await the influx of some spiritual tide for new combinations and correlations out of which will emerge a new art-form altogether: the art of the theater, already existent as a phrase, if not yet as a fact. It will involve the elements of mobility, form, color, and light, factors of which we cannot even guess the potency, because they are still in process of development.

The number and diversity of ways in which the

theater is related to the life of the time is the measure of its power to enrich and minister to that life. The medieval abbey was not only a gathering place for human beings for the worship of God, but also an inn, a school, a court, a farm, a workshop, and many other things besides. So should the theater assume an analogous position by no other process other than becoming what it essentially is: a gathering place of human beings for the understanding of man. If everything related to the production of drama were made or developed in the theater, few departments of human interest and endeavor would need to be left out. In this altered relation to the community, and dominated by a different consciousness, the theater instead of being, as now, a place of passive absorption, would assume its rightful place and fulfill its proper function, that of being a center of beautiful, intense, and joyous life: a temple for the celebration of the mysteries of the spirit.

Although the factors which go to make up the theater of the future are known in a general way in advance, by which I mean the literary, æsthetic, and mechanical elements likely to be involved, we do not know the coefficients of these factors because their magnitude depends on consciousness, and the consciousness within and behind the theater as a temple of humanity is bound to be utterly different from and superior to that behind the theater as a mirror of the preferences of the mere moment, or as a money-making institution.

The consciousness behind any theater is necessarily determined by some *master mind* from which everything takes its "shape and sun-color," and it is impossible to conceive of the theater as a temple without someone in the relation to it of minister or priest, one who, however little he might resemble the "cowled churchman," is possessed by that faith of which Emerson said:

> The word unto the prophet spoken
> Was writ on tables yet unbroken;
> The word of seers or sibyls told
> In groves of oak, or fanes of gold,
> Still floats upon the morning wind,
> Still whispers to the willing mind.

Next in importance to the hierophant would come that relatively small group of utterly dedicated devotees to whom the theater has become a shell in which *The Word* may be heard through and above the murmur of the world. The antechamber of this inner chamber would naturally be filled with workers of varied talents and of various sorts, related to

the first group as the hand is related to the brain, or
the will to the imagination. Next in order would be
the communicants, the "hearers" in the Pythagorean sense, and finally the congregation or audience.

Those individuals and groups which form this
whole would be dominated by a certain consciousness to which the ordinary axioms of mathematics
would not apply. In the noumenal world, or world
of causes, a whole may be greater than the sum of
its parts. So, given a group of people united by a
common devotion, such as the theater as a temple
is fully able to inspire, a flame of creative energy
might easily be engendered from the amicable fric-
tion of so many one-pointed minds. A new dimension might be added to consciousness through such
interaction of groups and individuals, all sublimated
by a common enthusiasm, quite in analogy with the
development of ecstasy by means of religious cere-
monies and ritualistic dances in which each partici-
pant has an allotted part to play.

Then, the contagion of such a group consciousness having been communicated to another larger
and differently constituted group, related to the first
as audience to actors, phenomena might conceivably
result of quite a different order from anything within
our customary experience, and with the descent of

demos, thus invoked, we might not only understand but experience *true* democracy. These great, primal, orgiastic tides of thought and feeling, the arousing and directing of which into beneficent channels was the *raison d'être* of the Mysteries and of the Mass, are practically unknown in modern life, or when known are allowed to waste themselves on the brutalities of the prize ring and the trivialities of the football and baseball fields. Perhaps our nearest approach to the strange intoxication of multitudes is to be found in the revival meeting and the political convention, manifestations more nearly subhuman than superhuman.

But in this mergence of many consciousnesses into one there dwells some mysterious, tremendous force, perilously poised between creation and destruction —diabolism and ecstacy. This force, of which we are either incredulous or afraid, is even now beating at the country's door, and it will enter either as mob-violence as a result of repression, or contrariwise, as a constructive, creative, spiritual outpouring. But to be this, it must have a prepared and natural channel such as the theater—swept clear of its accumulated rubbish, and lighted by a different consciousness— almost alone affords.

XI

FOOTPRINTS OF THE ETERNAL FUGITIVE

THIS LECTURE IS ABOUT THE TRACINGS MADE ON TIME and space by that which is timeless and spaceless—that "clothed eternity," the Life Force, which ripens women's breasts and makes hair grow on men's cheeks like grass, though it is itself formless, voiceless, sexless:

> It is not woman, neither is it man;
> It hastens without feet, sees without eyes;
> Time ne'er will finish it, it ne'er began;
> Greater than great, smaller than small, its size.

Or let us call it simply Nature. Although the language of Nature is infinitely various, she conveys always the same message. As Francis Thompson says: "Nature is but an imperfect actress, whose constant changes of dress never change her manner and method, who is the same in all her parts." We are blind to this uniformity, these similarities between things apparently unrelated, because of differences in material, medium, spatial magnitude, and temporal duration, but if we look about us, forgetting our clocks and our tape-measures, the statement that

Nature is the same in all her parts will be found to be deeply true. And with the study of Nature let us include also Art, because Art is Nature carried to a higher power by reason of its passage through a human consciousness, and become more articulate for that reason. For the aim of Art is to reveal transcendent glimpses of a divine order and harmony vouchsafed to the poet and mystic in their moments of vision. Let us, therefore, study the footprints of the Eternal Fugitive in Nature and Art, seeking, through the *world-aspect*, the *world-order*—those laws which govern all *becoming* in time and space.

The first truth everywhere published is the law of *unity*—oneness, myriad in manifestation, Nature is discovered to be "alike in all her parts." Atom and universe, man and the world—each is a unit, an organic and coherent whole. This is so obvious as to be unnecessary of elucidation. And what is true of Nature is also true of Art, for to say that a work of art must possess unity, must seem to proceed from a single impulse, and must be the embodiment of one dominant idea is to state a truism.

The second law, not contradicting but supplementing the first, is the law of *polarity*, i.e., duality. All things have sex, are either masculine or feminine. This is the handwriting on space of one of those transcendental truths of the Ancient Wisdom, namely, that the Logos, in voluntarily circumscribing His infinite life for purpose of manifestation, encloses Himself within His limiting veil, maya, and that His life appears as spirit (male), and as matter (female)—name and form. The two terms of this polarity are endlessly repeated throughout Nature: in sun and moon, day and night, fire and water, man and woman—and so on. A close interrelation is seen to subsist between corresponding members of such pairs of opposites: sun, day, fire, man expresses the primal and active aspect of the Eternal Fugitive; moon, night, water, woman, its secondary or passive aspect. Moreover, each one implies or brings to mind the others of its class: man, like the sun, is lord of day; he is like fire, a devastating force, centrifugal; woman is subject to the lunar rhythm; like water, she is fecund, sinuous, centripetal.

It is desirable to have an instant and keen realization of this sex quality, and to make this easier, think of those things which are allied to time as masculine, and to space as feminine: as motion and matter, mind and body, and so forth. The English words "masculine" and "feminine" are too intimately associated in consciousness with the idea of physical sex to designate properly the two terms of this polar-

146

ity. In Japanese philosophy and art (derived from the Chinese) they are called *In* and *Yo* (*In*, feminine, *Yo*, masculine), and these little words, being free from the limitations of their English correlatives, will be found convenient. *Yo* is used to designate that which is simple, direct, primary, active, positive; and *In*, that which is complex, indirect, derivative, passive, negative. Things hard, straight, fixed, vertical, are *Yo*; things curved, soft, horizontal, fluctuating, are *In*.

In passing I may say that the superiority of the line, mass, and color composition of Chinese paintings and Japanese prints and kakemonos to that of the vastly more pretentious easel pictures of Occidental artists—a superiority now generally acknowledged by connoisseurs—is largely due to the conscious following, on the part of the Orientals, of this principle of sex-complementaries.

Nowhere are *In* and *Yo* more simply and adequately imaged than in the vegetable kingdom. The trunk of a tree is *Yo*, its foliage, *In*; and in each stem and leaf the two are repeated. A calla, consisting of a single straight and rigid spadix, embraced within a soft and tenderly curved spathe, affords an admirable expression of the characteristic differences between *In* and *Yo* and their reciprocal relation. The

147

two are not often combined in such perfection in a single form. Trees such as the pine and hemlock, which are *excurrent*—those in which the branches start successively (i.e., after the manner of time) from a straight and vertical central stem—are *Yo*; trees such as the elm and the willow, which are *deliquescent*—those in which the trunk dissolves as it were simultaneously (after the manner of space) into its branches—are *In*. All tree forms lie in or between these two extremes, and leaves are susceptible of a similar classification. Succession, which is of time, is expressed by elements arranged with relation to axial lines; simultaneousness, which is of space, by elements arranged with relation to focal points. Learn to look at nature in this way, and to recognize *In* and *Yo* in all their protean present-ments—in the cloud upon the mountain, the wave against the cliff, the tracery of trees etched on the sky.

This concept of *twoness*, polarity, should now be modified by another, namely—*trinity*. For in every duality a third is latent. Each sex is in process of becoming the other, and this alternation is accomplished by means of a third term or neuter, which is unlike either of the original two in that it partakes of the nature of them both, just as a child may re-

Skyscrapers of Rockefeller Center, New York, seen through the armillary sphere crowning Lee Lawrie's statue of Atlas.

semble both its parents. Twilight comes between day and night; earth is the child of fire and water; in music, besides the chord of longing and striving, and the chord of rest and fulfillment (the dominant seventh and the tonic) there is a third, or resolving chord in which the two are reconciled. In the sacred syllable Om (Aum), which epitomizes all speech, the u sound effects a transition between the a sound, one of suspense, and the m sound, one of satisfaction. Among the primary colors, green comes between red and blue; and in architecture, the arch, which is both weight and support, which is neither vertical nor horizontal, may be considered the neuter of the group of which the column and the lintel are respectively masculine and feminine. "These are the three, the only three letters from which has been expanded the architectural art, as a great and superb language, through which man has expressed, through the generations, the changing drift of his thoughts." These three elements of vertical, horizontal, and curved, are combined in the ansated cross of the Egyptians, the Buddhist wheel, the fylfot inscribed within a circle, and those numerous Christian symbols combining the circle and the cross. We of today are not given to discovering anything wonderful in these ideographs, done with three strokes of a pen, but they are full of profound meanings nevertheless.

The fourth footprint of the Eternal Fugitive to which I would call your attention is the law of consonance, expressed in the phrase: "As is the small, so is the great: as is the outer, so is the inner." This is a succinct statement of a fundamental and far-reaching truth. The scientist recognizes it now and then and here and there, but the occultist always and utterly. To him the microcosm and the macrocosm are one and the same in essence, and the forthgoing impulse which calls a universe into being and the indrawing impulse which extinguishes it again —the days and nights of Brahman, each lasting millions of years—are echoed and repeated in the inflow and outflow of the breath through the nostrils, in nutrition and excretion, in daily activity and nightly rest.

In the same way, in Nature, a thing is echoed and repeated throughout its parts. Each leaf on a tree is itself a tree in miniature, each blossom a modified leaf; every vertebrate animal is a complicated system of spines; the ripple is the wave of a larger wave, and that larger wave is part of the ebbing and flowing tide. In music this law is illustrated in the return of the tonic to itself in the octave, and in its partial return in the dominant; also, in a more extended sense, in the repetition of a major theme in the minor, or in the treble and again in the bass, with perhaps other modifications of time and key. In the art of painting the law of consonance is exemplified in the repetition with variation of certain colors and combinations of lines in different parts of the same picture. Every painter knows that any important color in his picture must be echoed in different places for the success of the whole. Every pinnacle of a Gothic cathedral is a little tower with its spire; the great vault of the cathedral nave, together with the pointed roof above it is repeated in the entrance arch with its gable, and the same two elements appear in every statue-enshrining niche. Thus in a work of art, as in a piece of tapestry, the same thread runs through the web, but goes to make up different figures. There is one life, but many manifestations; hence, inevitably, echoes, resemblances—*consonances*.

Another principle of natural beauty, closely allied to the law of consonance, is that of *diversity in monotony*—not identity, but difference, showing itself for the most part as perceptible and piquant variation between individual units belonging to the same class, type, or species. No two trees put forth their branches in just the same manner, and no two leaves from the same tree exactly correspond. No two persons look alike though they have similar members and features; even the markings of the skin of the thumb are different in every human hand.

Every principle of natural beauty is but the presentment of some occult law, and this one proclaims that identity does not exclude difference, that individuality need not be smothered in uniformity. In architecture this is admirably suggested in the metopes of the frieze of the Parthenon. Seen at a distance, these must have presented a scarcely distinguishable texture of sunlit marble and cool shadow, yet in reality each is a separate work of art. In Gothic cathedrals, in Romanesque monastery cloisters, a teeming variety of invention is hidden beneath a surface uniformity, and the same spirit of controlled individuality, of liberty subservient to the law of all, is illustrated in the capitals of the columns of the wonderful sea-arcade of the Venetian Ducal palace: alike in general contour, they differ widely, and together unfold a Bible story.

If one were to establish an axial plane vertically through the center of a tree, it would be found that the masses of foliage, however irregularly shaped on

either side of such an axis, just about balanced one
another. Similarly, in all our bodily movements, with
every change of position there occurs an opposition
of members of such a nature that an axial plane
through the center of gravity would divide the body
into two substantially equal masses. This physical
plane law of balance corresponds to the law of karma, or compensation; on the plane metaphysical,
whereby all accounts are squared—it is Justice, aptly
symbolized by the scales.

Balance finds abundant illustration in art: in music by the opposition of one phrase by another; in
painting by the disposition of forms and colors so
that they complement and compensate one another.
In architecture the law of balance is observed in a
symmetrical disposition of parts, at its best when the
opposed elements do not exactly "match," as in the
twin towers of Chartres and of Amiens, for example.
This sort of balance is characteristic of Gothic architecture, as mere symmetry is characteristic of Classic.

There is observable in Nature a universal tendency
toward refinement and compactness of form in space;
or contrariwise, toward increment and diffusion,
manifested in time as acceleration or retardation. It
is governed, in either case, by an exact mathematical
law, like the law of falling bodies. It shows itself in

the widening circles which appear when one drops a stone in still water, in the convolutions of shells, in the branching of trees, and the veining of leaves; the diminution on the sizes of the pipes of an organ illustrates it, and the spacing of the frets of a guitar. This *rhythmic diminution* is everywhere, because it is in the eye itself, for any series of mathematically equal units, such as the columns and inter-columnations of a colonnade, becomes when viewed in perspective rhythmically unequal, diminishing according to the universal law.

The final principle of natural beauty to which I would call your attention is the law of *radiation*, which in some sort is a return to the first, the law of *unity*. The various parts of any organism radiate from, or otherwise refer back to common centers or foci. The law is represented in its simplicity in the starfish—in its complexity in the body of man, himself a sort of starfish, but with foci also in the brain and in the heart. A tree is centered in the seed, and a solar system, in its sun.

Here are nine footprints of the Eternal Fugitive, and there are others. It is not their multiplicity and diversity which is important, but rather their relatedness and coördination, for they are all aspects of that whereby the Life Force manifests itself in time and space. Let me make this correlation plain, and at the same time fix what has gone before more firmly.

First comes the law of *Unity*; then, since every unit is in essence twofold, there is the law of *Polarity*. But this duality is not static, but dynamic, the two poles acting and reacting upon one another to produce a third, hence, the law of *Trinity*. Given this third term and the innumerable combinations made possible by its relations to and reactions upon the original pair, the law of *Multiplicity in Unity* naturally follows, as does the law of *Consonance* or repetition, since the primal process of differentiation repeats itself, and the original combinations reappear—but reappear in changed form, hence the law of *Diversity*. The law of *Balance* naturally follows, and because all things are waxing and waning, there is the law of *Rhythmic Change*. *Radiation* rediscovers and reaffirms, even amid the utmost complexity, that essential and fundamental unity from which the complexity was wrought.

Everything obeys and illustrates one or another of these laws, so ubiquitous are they, and so inseparable from every kind of manifestation in time and space. It is the number of them which finds illustration within small compass which makes for beauty, because beauty is the fine flower of a sort of sublime ingenuity. A work of art is nothing, if not *artful*: like an acrostic, the more different ways it can be read—up, down, across, from right to left, from left to right—the better it is, other things being equal. The extent to which a work of art is filled with meaning beyond meaning, the greater its chance of survival, the more powerful its appeal. For enjoyment it is not necessary that all these meanings should be fathomed, for by the deeper consciousness they will be *felt*.

XII

THE GIFT OF ASIA
A Dialogue

IT IS SUMMER IN THE ADIRONDACKS. THE DISK OF
THE RISING SUN IS JUST APPEARING ABOVE THE SHOUL-
DER OF THE MOUNTAIN, WHICH ENFOLDS WITH ITS
LONG ARM OF SHADOW THE SLEEPING LAKE.

IN A RUSTIC KIOSK TWO MEN, A POET AND AN ACTOR,
STAND SPELLBOUND AT THE GROWING GLORY OF THE
SUNRISE WHICH LIKE A TORCH LIGHTS UP TIER AFTER
TIER OF DISTANT TREES.

PRESENTLY, THE POET TAKES A BOOK OUT OF HIS
COAT POCKET, SEATS HIMSELF, AND BEGINS TO READ.

THE ACTOR: (A LITTLE SCORNFULLY) *Why do you
bury your nose in a book at this hour and in this
place? Has the sunrise already begun to bore you?*

THE POET: (ABSENTLY) *The sunrise is here; in this
book—and in my heart.*

THE ACTOR: (SURPRISED AND A TRIFLE DISCONCERTED)
And just what do you mean by that?

THE POET: *The sun, you know, never rises. You
have succumbed to an ancient illusion. You are*

aware, I take it, that it is only the axial movement of the earth which has brought our hemisphere into an ever-existent light?

THE ACTOR: Of course, but that doesn't answer my question. Besides, you contradict yourself. The sunrise in your book and heart—isn't that an illusion too?

THE POET: (ORACULARLY) Yes, for many an eager heart today there is the illusion of a sun having risen because the soul's dark hemisphere has wheeled into the ever-shining Presence after a night of troubled sleep. The spiritual light of the world, like sunlight, streams forth from the East. That light is in this book, which contains the stored-up wisdom of the East.

THE ACTOR: (WITH SOME IMPATIENCE) Why should a good American like you go to such far, strange sources for inspiration? Have you exhausted all that there is in the teachings of Christ?

THE POET: I might retort that Christ was himself an Oriental, but I'll content myself with saying that in my opinion the West has so ignored or misconceived Christ's message that in order to understand it aright we must go back to the pure source whence it came.

THE ACTOR: (WITH SUPPRESSED SARCASM) And what may that be, according to your notion?

THE POET: The Ancient Wisdom of the Aryan race. For as the Aryan is the source of European races, and its language, the Sanskrit, the source of our modern languages, so is the ancient religion of India the fecund mother of all the religions which have since appeared in the world.

THE ACTOR: (INCREDULOUSLY) Do you mean to tell me that all religions are the same?

THE POET: Exoterically, no; esoterically, yes. All the differences between religions are differences of form and not of content—colorations caused by the mind of man, refractions of the white light of truth implanted in his inner consciousness since the beginning of his life on earth.

THE ACTOR: (AT LAST INTERESTED IN SPITE OF HIMSELF) And why have we lost this truth, since I infer that you think we have lost it?

THE POET: We have not lost it: it has been only overlooked and overlaid. In the strange narrowness of mid-Victorian materialism we had come to conceive of the world as a laboratory full of things awaiting identification and classification. We were

industriously proceeding to affix the proper labels
and arrange the bottles when something happened—
to some of us, I mean—the birth of wonder. Then
the labels all seemed silly or meaningless, and the
bottles broke in our hands. In the air of that mysterious morning, amid the wreckage of our system, did
we interrogate the dark. There was a period of suspense, of wonder—then light broke in the East.

THE ACTOR: (AGAIN SARCASTIC) When you say "we"
for whom are you speaking? Not for me, surely, or
you wouldn't be speaking to me. And when, pray,
did this great event occur? I've seen no reference to
it in any newspaper; it hasn't been made into a play
or a tale.

THE POET: I speak for those to whom the Ancient
Wisdom of the East became the particular sun of
their salvation, and its dawning occurred—so strange
are the ways of the Masters of Wisdom—when their
faithful disciple, Helena Petrovna Blavatsky, brought
the Gift of Asia to this land, destined to bring forth
in travail the sons and daughters of a great new race.

THE ACTOR: (PUZZLED BUT INTERESTED) And what
is this "Gift of Asia"? I confess I quite fail to understand.

THE POET: The oldest and greatest of all sciences:

the science of release. Now release, the Upanishads say, exists in the soul like the quality of clearness in a mirror. Cleanse the mirror, and it reflects an image; so, in the soul, beneath the karmic accumulation of centuries of vain self-seeking, there is ever the quality of clearness which will one day reveal the divine image and bring release from the round of births and deaths. For the soul bears in itself its own salvation; it has no need of ritual or observance, or for the midwifery of minister or priest.

THE ACTOR: (IMPRESSED IN SPITE OF HIMSELF) *That is beautiful, and somehow familiar, though I can't say I ever heard it put in just that way before. Go on, tell me more.*

THE POET: (WARMING TO HIS SUBJECT) *According to the ancient teaching, man is himself the Eternal Thinker, thinking non-eternal thoughts. The Self in man, the Knower, the Enjoyer, being one with the All-Self, or "Father in Heaven," is not born, nor does it die. That which we call birth is but the assumption, by an immortal individual, of the physical limitation of a perishable personality for the purpose of tasting a certain order of experience. That which we call death is the withdrawal from the self-imposed limitation—no more an end than birth is a beginning.*

You are an actor. Well, just as at the end of a play you lay aside, with the clothes you have worn, the character you were assuming, and forgetting for a time the part and the playhouse, you resume your own true life, never really intermitted, so at the death of the body the immortal individual dissipates the transitory personality which it has projected out of eternity into time.

THE ACTOR: And does this thing go on indefinitely; does the "immortal individual" incarnate again and again just as I return to the theater night after night, assuming different roles on different nights?

THE POET: Exactly! The Ego—in some mysterious way one with the All—is related to its personal mani-festations much as you are related to the characters of your repertoire. It appears again and again upon the lighted stage of the world in different bodies—masks, as it were, for you must remember that the word persona means a mask—for enrichment, for enjoyment, for self-realization. This is the play of Brahm: you are Brahm, I am Brahm, we are all Brahm.

THE ACTOR: Then why can we not remember our incarnations, just as I remember my parts?

THE POET: *In our free state, in eternity, we do re-member—or rather, we realize, for the past exists now. When we have mastered life we shall remember, for there are those who are able to do this even now. But for the most part we are too immersed in the precarious business of living to be conscious of aught else, and besides, now the knowledge would bring us nothing but distress. To have recourse again to our analogy, you yourself once told me that a good actor "psychologizes" his part; that is, he so identifies his consciousness with the character he is called upon to portray as to experience the thoughts and emotions native to it, and the vicissitudes of its life become his own. That he may more truly real-ize and render a fiction he permits it for the time being to hold sway over his soul. Only at the fall of the final curtain does he permit the memory of all that he has shut out to flow back into his con-sciousness. Even so are we overcome by the illusions of the world.*

THE ACTOR: (ADMIRINGLY) *Well, I must say that's a clever way of presenting the idea of reincarnation to a man of my calling. But you do not mean to tell me that it's all put so neatly and completely there in your sacred book of the East?*

163

THE POET: (WITH ENTHUSIASM) *It is stated far better than I can state it. Listen!* (HE READS) "And as a goldsmith, taking a piece of gold, turns it into another newer and more beautiful shape, so does this Self, after having thrown off this body and dispelled all ignorance, make unto himself another newer and more beautiful shape." And listen to this: "An eternal portion of me it is, which becoming an individual soul in the mortal world, draws the senses and the mind as a sixth." That is to say, in order to function in a world such as ours—the three-dimensional world—a physical body is necessary. The higher Self, through and by means of the psyche, organizes such a body and brings it to birth through ordinary generation. Throughout the life-cycle of this body it is tempered into an ever finer, firmer, and more sensitive vehicle for knowledge, for self-expression, for enjoyment. When the higher Self has worn out one such vehicle it destroys it and builds and animates others until the soul has learned the precious secret of RELEASE.

THE ACTOR: (PUZZLED) *Release—I don't know just what you mean by release.*

THE POET: *Sleep is release, death is release, for in those states the soul returns to its immortal source,* but the Great Release is that which liberates from the round of births and deaths, and many lives are required for its achievement. (READS) "If a man cannot understand it before the falling asunder of the body, then he has to take bodies again in the world of creation."

THE ACTOR: (EAGERLY) And how may one come to understand it?

THE POET: To understand it is to recognize no reality but the All Self; to realize that Self as individualized in us; to look upon sin, sickness, suffering as illusions of the personality, the products of ignorance and limitation.

THE ACTOR: That sounds suspiciously like Christian Science. It certainly reduces life to a very simple formula: too simple, for how then do you account for that ceaseless warfare between good and ignoble impulses which is the very texture of life itself, and the reality of which it is impossible to question?

THE POET: The Ancient wisdom accounts for this conflict in a manner curiously in accord with the ideas of Schopenhauer, who by his own avowal was deeply indebted to Eastern philosophy. The parallel is so striking that I have copied here what Schopenhauer wrote. (READS) "*The one will which objecti-fies itself in all ideas always seeks the highest possi-ble objectification, and has therefore in this case given up the lower grades of its manifestation after a conflict: since a higher idea or objectification of will can only appear through a lower, it endures the opposition of these lower ideas, which, though brought into subjection, will strive to obtain an in-dependent and complete expression of their being.*"

These husks of the embodied Self, the wraiths of old thoughts, old habits, old desires, grasp at it with ghostly fingers in order to repeat the old delight. They are like the succubi of the Middle Ages, which in the semblance of beautiful women visited young men in their sleep and then disintegrated before their eyes. Thus do the living strive ever against the vampire embraces of their dead. It has been said that the devil is composed of God's ruins—the only antagonist of the soul is that which it was yesterday.

THE ACTOR: How do you explain what we Chris-tians call "sin," and have you anything in your sys-tem which corresponds to what we name the cruci-fixion and the redemption—I use these words in their mystical sense—and to those other hallowed and familiar ideas embodied in what I shall have to

call "enlightened" Christianity to distinguish it
from old-fashioned orthodoxy?

THE POET: The body, organized and animated by
the soul or psychic nature, is composed of that "elemental essence" polarized downward toward form
rather than upward toward spirit: the father of this
flesh was the fire-mist, its mother was water, and in
obedience to the law of its being it is hastening toward those forms, states, and conditions which the
psyche has long ago transcended and left behind.
Only by overcoming this downward tendency of its
vehicle can the soul "redeem" its world, which is the
body. Hence it must immerse itself, must crucify
itself upon the cross of materiality in order to wash
out the "sins" of that world. This crucifixion is the
price of redemption. Its peril is lest the divine fragment will itself be drawn—for a time—into the vor-
tex of the descending stream, and so forget its Âtma
or "Father in Heaven."

In the confluence of these two contending streams,
of sense and soul—in this love which is warfare and
this warfare which is love—a lower, or reflex personality is engendered which in the literature of Eastern
philosophy is given the name of the elemental self.
Oriental imagery is taxed to the utmost to make

plain the difference between the higher Self, "without passion and without parts," and its inverted and distorted counterpart, the elemental self, a plexus of irrational impulses and desires; for in a right understanding of this difference lies the solution of our problem, the way out of our human predicament.

THE ACTOR: (A LITTLE ANXIOUSLY) I am afraid I do not get clearly this distinction upon which you say everything depends.

THE POET: Listen, then. This is the way the higher Self is described in the Upanishads. (READS) "In the highest golden sheath there is Brahman, without passion and without parts . . . When he is in union with the body, the senses and the mind, then wise people call him the Enjoyer . . . He is pure, firm, stable, undefiled, unmoved, free from desire, resting in himself."

The elemental self, on the other hand, is thus described: (READS) "There is indeed that other, different one, called the elemental self, who, overcome with bright and dark fruit of action, enters a good or bad birth. . . . He is overcome by the qualities of nature. Then because he is thus overcome, he becomes bewildered, and because he is bewildered he sees not the creator, the holy Lord, abiding within himself. Carried along by the waves of the qualities, unstable, fickle, crippled, full of desires, vacillating, he enters into belief: believing 'I am he, this is mine,' he binds his self with his self as a bird with a net.''

This, then, is the quintessence of the Eastern teaching: the infinite exists potentially in every being. The Great Self without Selfishness is the only reality. The elemental self is a falsity, an illusion, a mirage. The realization of its ephemeral and illusory nature brings about the disintegration of the false self; as the sun sucks up the eye-deceiving vapor so does the aroused consciousness penetrate veil after veil until the infinite vision comes. This reversal of the poles of consciousness whereby release is attained is "that far-off, divine event toward which the whole creation moves." It is the crowning achievement of innumerable effortful lives.

THE SUN, NOW FULLY RISEN, BANISHES THE MOUNTAIN'S SHADOW AND BURNISHES THE LAKE WITH GOLD. BOTH MEN SIT ABSORBED IN THE CONTEMPLATION OF THE FAMILIAR MIRACLE OF THE RELEASE OF EARTH FROM THE BONDAGE OF DARKNESS. THE BOOK SLIPS FROM THE POET'S HAND. THE ACTOR TAKES IT UP AND BEGINS TO SLOWLY TURN ITS PAGES.

XIII

THE RITUAL OF PLAY

AN INCORRIGIBLE SYMBOLIST, I HAVE AN IDEA THAT children might be given a certain kind of so-called spiritual instruction through the mediumship of their toys and their games. These things become to them, all unconsciously, the very ritual of their worship: this is why playing children, like praying mystics, though happy, are of so serious a mien.

Most children are naturally religious in the psychological, not the theological, sense of the word. Their souls open to true transcendentalism as naturally as flowers open to the sun. It would seem as though they had only to be reminded, rather than taught, of life's more profound meanings.

Now that instruction is always the most apt and enduring which awakens interest and delight, and, since the child's interest and delight are in his play, here is a prepared and natural channel which can be utilized, in many different ways.

The following interpretation of children's toys and games makes no pretense of being exhaustive, neither are the meanings assigned anything more than suggestive, for every symbol, from the very nature of symbolism, may mean many things. All that has been attempted is to make the point, by means of illustrative examples, that children's play is highly symbolic, with the idea of inspiring parents and teachers themselves to perceive *and in their own way interpret* these to the child. This should have the effect of stimulating the growth of certain fine flowers of the mind and spirit even while the little hands and brains are engaged in mastering the mere machinery of life.

DOLLS: The body is but the doll of the higher nature, for without the constant ministrations of its divine mistress the body is only a stuffed and colored image, its flesh no better than wax, its bones than sawdust. Just as a child plays with its dolls, so does the Self attend the body, determining, directing, and manipulating the manifold activities of its "reflex personality."

Teach the child by means of this symbol that as it loves and cares for its doll, so is it loved and cared for by the divine part of its own nature.

KITES: A kite is an ambition to achieve the Highest, held firmly against the buffeting winds of circumstance by the strong string of common sense. Sometimes it is hard to get a kite into the air; again and again it tumbles; but once aloft it easily rides the breezes, going, like a good habit, of itself. The great thing in a kite is to have it properly balanced. This is a matter of adjustment, and adjustment to the different demands of everyday life is what saves the high-soaring aspirations from disastrous plunges and falls.

Teach the child by means of this symbol that as it walks the ways of earth it should send up to God some part of its nature, to be held aloft there, serene and calm.

TOPS: We are all tops set spinning from the hand of God. What we call our life, our sustained rotation about the point of personality, is but His love. Because, like the top's motion, this life inheres in us, we cannot think of it as other than our own.

Teach the child by means of this symbol that just as the top can stand only so long as it is in motion, activity and effort keep the soul fixed and firm amid the illusions and temptations of the world.

QUOITS: The stake is Ambition; the rings are Opportunity. To excel in pitching quoits it is necessary to regard each ring pitched as the only one, focusing all attention and effort upon that. So in life, to attain any ambition, each opportunity must seem to be the last.

Teach the child by means of this symbol that the skill gained in many abortive efforts paves the way to ultimate success; that concentration should be cultivated at all costs.

THE RETURN-BALL: (A ring for the finger to which is attached an elastic cord and, on the other end of the cord, a ball.)

The child's hand is the bosom of the Father; the ring is the human spirit forever in union with the Most High. The ball is that eager and adventurous desire-nature which flies forth questing experience and would return never but for the soul—the stretched string—attached both to heaven, its home, and to earth, its lodging-place for a night. The soul follows the sense-nature so that when the outgoing impulse slackens it may bring the prodigal back home.

Teach the child by means of this symbol that into whatever hell of suffering he in his sightlessness may wander, there is always that in him through which he may attain the Light.

BALL: A ball is a thought: it flies wherever it is

directed, to a distance and with a velocity proportional to the power which propelled it. If a ball is thrown too high, it falls short; if it is thrown too low, it hits the ground, and, diverted by obstacles, may not reach its destination. In like manner, if one's thoughts soar too far above the earth they lose in practical efficiency, while if they fly low they are diverted by every trivial circumstance.

Teach the child by means of this symbol that while he is learning to throw a ball swift and straight, to catch it with certainty, and to return it nimbly, so in sending out thoughts he should be accurate and forceful, and in receiving the thoughts of others he should be alert and receptive. Teach him that just as he must keep his eye upon the ball, so must he keep his mind upon the thought.

FIREWORKS: Pick apart your bomb or rocket—carefully though!—what do you find? Ugly gray powder, little black things like stones, strings perhaps, and a paper fuse or two. Yet out of this scant handful of seemingly dirty rubbish can come sound great enough to drown out thunder, light bright enough to eclipse for a moment the arrayed constellations of the sky. And all that is required to liberate this latent beauty is a little spark of fire.

Though in our unillumined moments we seem to ourselves such poor and pitiful creatures, there is a dynamic power in us, which, released by some spark of love or aspiration, may "magnify the Universal Soul" to the amazement of mankind.

Teach the child by means of this symbol that, fired by some noble passion, the heart of the humblest may blaze forth into transcendent beauty like a rocket in the night.

THE HUMMING WHEEL: (A hollow tin wheel with two holes in it hung on this double axis in the middle of a loop of soft string; alternately tightening and slackening this at the right intervals, the wheel is made to revolve rapidly backward and forward. When it attains a certain speed it gives forth a musical note.)

The wheel is a symbol of the terrestrial nature. The soul—the string—communicates to it the rhythm of its life-movement and so converts an inert and voiceless thing into a harmoniously vibrating vehicle.

Teach the child by means of this symbol that if it would hear the song of life it must discover and obey the rhythm of life.

THE SKIPPING ROPE: The skipper leaps at those intervals established by the revolving rope: if he jumps a moment too soon or too late the rope will trip him.

We should seek to discover and respond to those cyclic movements of the inner self by means of which we are able to transcend the plane of every-day existence. But if we attempt to precipitate those moments of illumination, or to prolong them beyond their natural term, we lose the sense of that inner rhythm.

Teach the child by means of this symbol that in life, as in rope-skipping, the secret of success is to seize, but never to overstay, the opportune moment for action.

STRING FIGURES (The Cat's Cradle): A piece of string is perhaps the simplest of all playthings, and the most universal. The invention and manipulation of string figures is a favorite amusement in all parts of the world. This diversion is popular not alone among children, savages, and peasants, but among highly civilized and serious-minded men and women who exchange their inventions in the same way that chess players exchange chess problems. Learned articles have been written and books have been published on the subject of string figures until it has risen to the dignity of a cult.

Teach the child by means of this symbol that it is not so much the richness of his endowment that matters, as the use he may be able to make of any talent, however meager, of which he stands possessed.

JACK STRAWS: It is impossible to excel at the game of Jack Straws unless all one's attention and effort are centered upon releasing one straw at one time. Hesitancy at the wrong moment, or the attempt to release two straws from the pile in a single trial, is apt to spell disaster. This game is an apt symbol of the complex life of today and of the manner with which it should be dealt. Each morning sees us confronted with a heaped pile of tasks, duties, problems, responsibilities, solicitations of every sort. Success depends on our wisdom in choosing, and, having chosen, the single-mindedness we are able to bring to the particular thing in hand. Failure is sure to follow if in attempting one thing we cannot help thinking about another, or if we try to do too many things at once.

Teach the child by means of this symbol that sureness, deftness, concentration, so necessary for the trivial game of Jack Straws, are not less necessary in the great game of life.

177

STILTS: If a man essay to elevate himself artificially above the level of ordinary humanity on the stilts of a special morality, he is in a state of unstable equilibrium: his only chance of sustaining himself in this position, like that of the stilt-walker, is in balance, in unceasing shifting about.

Teach the child by means of this symbol that, if he sets himself up as superior to other children, he is in constant danger of a fall.

HIDE AND SEEK: In the game of Hide and Seek, the child, after an interval of "blinding," seeks out his scattered playmates one by one. So perhaps also does the soul, after the lethal interval of death, seek out those karmically linked to it, resuming and carrying forward relations established in antecedent lives.

Teach the child by means of this symbol that life is a seeking and a finding, a sport of the soul, interrupted but never ended, carried on with familiar, dear, immortal companions.

SNAP THE WHIP: In the game of Snap the Whip the secret of not being thrown when the jerk comes lies in holding tight to the hands of one's companions on either side.

In the great crises of life a man needs the sympathy and support of his friends, and he is sure of this only if he holds to them firmly and loyally at all times.

Teach the child by means of this symbol that in life, as in the game of Snap the Whip, the farther away one is from the leader the greater the danger of being thrown down and left behind.

SKATING: The act of skating is a process of falling, the fall being arrested by the skill of the skater in so adjusting the position of his body in relation to its center of gravity that the perpetually imperilled equilibrium is never irrecoverably lost. Learning to skate is therefore learning to fall and to recover in such rhythmic sequence, and with such certainty and swiftness, that when the art is once mastered delightful movements always forfend imminent disaster.

Teach the child by means of this symbol that in learning to live, as in learning to skate, there must not be too much fear of falling, for only by falling is it possible to learn at all.

FISHING: The suspense and excitement of fishing finds its analogue on the higher arc of life's spiral whenever the hook of desire is cast into the deep waters of potential experience. The stern joy of the struggle between the fisherman and the captive fish finds its parallel in the exultation which comes with the achievement of any desired object; and the feeling deep in the heart of the fisherman when he sees his spent victim gasping its life out corresponds to that distaste and disillusion which forever dogs the footsteps of gratified desire.

Teach the child that the fascinating and cruel sport of fishing is a thing to be experienced, perhaps, but in the end outgrown: just as that see-saw between wanting and getting the objects of desire, however native to the terrestrial nature, is neither native nor necessary to the soul, and is, therefore, to be outgrown.

SWIMMING: In swimming, perhaps, more than in any other sport, confidence is the prime requisite. The feeling that water will as easily sustain the body as engulf it is a great aid in learning to swim. This is shown by the fact that a beginner often succeeds in keeping himself afloat when he imagines he is being supported, but fails as soon as he discovers that his imagining was wrong. The swimmer must trust his medium, submerge his body to the utmost: the more he tries to keep himself above the water, the more violent must be his efforts to keep from going under.

Teach the child that in the life of the spirit there must be faith, there must be trust. God's love will sustain us always if we only believe that it will.

XIV

"WHERE ARE YOU GOING, MY PRETTY MAID?"

THIS IS AN INQUIRY INTO THE INTERESTS, ACTIVITIES, aspirations (if she has any), of the modern young woman, and an indication of the direction in which I think she should be headed. Her answer to the question: "Where are you going, my pretty maid?" would probably be, in the words of a once-popular song: "I don't know where I'm goin' but I'm on my way!" And on her way she certainly is, with that free stride of hers, so unlike the walk of the women of any country I have ever visited.

The truly significant movements and events often go unrecognized and unrecorded by the Historic Muse. One of these movements I believe to be the disturbance of the balance of power between the sexes in this country at the present time because of the economic independence of woman, and her intellectual freedom; today she controls more than half of the wealth of the nation, and she is the custodian of its culture. To her tastes all manufacturers and tradesmen have to cater; there is scarcely a field of activity which she has not invaded, the business world would become paralyzed without her; she is on the jury, in the Cabinet, and in Congress; education of the young is largely in her hands, and in the world of art and letters she is supreme arbiter. To these factors might be added what Bernard Shaw calls the "sterilization" of woman, by which he means the use of contra-conceptives for the purpose of escaping "the curse of Eve."

But there is another side to the picture: for the moment she is the victim of her own victory. Self-exiled from her ancient sanctuary, the dark shadow of her new freedom is her new loneliness. Escaped from bondage, questing every kind of knowledge and experience, she has outstripped her companion, man, caught in the whirring wheels of competitive industrialism. She is not understood by him in these new aspects; he resents them, and this has brought about in many cases an alienation deeper far than that caused by so-called marital infidelity.

This disturbance of an age-old equilibrium has disturbed woman's own equilibrium in such a way as to act adversely on a certain contingent. In the rude jostle of business, professional, or political life, some have lost their *femininité*, which is like an angel losing his halo, or a dove the iridescence of its breast. Others have become "hard-boiled," a thing no longer woman, nor yet man, but a neuter worker in the money-hive, intent upon maintaining that competitive, materialistic, militaristic civilization which it should be the modern woman's aim to regenerate and transform, or, failing in that, to undermine and destroy, because it makes men creatures of its mechanisms. Still others, with the removal of the ancient taboos, have become extravagant, dissolute, self-centered, and self-indulgent, flaunting the manners and morals of the underworld, and thus vulgarizing social life, which is no less a betrayal of their sex and a reversal of its function. Herein lies a great danger, for the psyche of woman is like the surface of water: she will reflect any image, but she can not reflect ugly, ignoble, or depraved images without doing violence to her essential nature. To be made to do so gives rise to that peculiar kind of subjective suffering which so afflicts many women now-a-days without their knowing either its cause or its cure. For psychically woman is constituted to bring to birth a certain kind of supernal beauty. She it is who forces the thorny stalk of life to put forth blossoms; indeed, it would scarcely be an exaggeration to say that woman's part in the work of civilization is so great that the entire edifice is reared on the shoulders of these "frail caryatids." For in the beginning, while man went forth to hunt and fight, woman remained to plait and weave and mold those coverings and containers in which all the arts and crafts had their origin, and afterwards, and at all times, she fecundates man's imagination and inspires his creativeness through her beauty, her mystery, and the miracle of her tenderness.

The occult reason for this struggle of the modern woman for more room to move about is that she may fulfill a new evolutionary function, which is the bringing to birth in human consciousness of a new faculty, the intuition, as a valid means of apprehension. Woman is more intuitional than man, he being muscular, and she, glandular. If, as seems probable, the intuition is the next human faculty to be developed—as the power to reason and form concepts was the last one—woman occupies at the present time a position of unique, of supreme importance.

Again I would remind you that the only evolution is the evolution of consciousness. Upon it even the dimensionality of space depends. We are now in the third stage of consciousness-development, the so-called age of reason; but because some have already entered on the fourth stage on account of the emergence in them of the faculty of intuition, those in whom it is actively operating find themselves increasingly aware of the four-dimensional world. This accounts better than anything else for the invasion of the mystical, the miraculous, the magical, which is such an outstanding phenomenon of these times, things which orthodox religion and classical science combat in vain. It accounts also for the prevalence of psychism among women. Of psychic women I know and have known many, and I was married to one for seven years. The matter was first forced on my attention when I became the president of a Theosophical lodge, for cults of this kind are, as you know, preponderately feminine. They become the refuge of women who, by reason of the thinning of the veil between this work-a-day world and the world of the wondrous, have been subject to experiences the reality of which they can not question, for which their spiritual guides offer no panacea except condemnation, and all references to which are received by their families and friends with incredulity, irritation, or contempt. The pressure of such unprecedented emotional experiences upon persons of undisciplined wills, and new ideas fermenting in minds unprepared to receive them, create conditions which take on the appearance of disease, mental or

186

physical. For this reason these women become the victims of horrible malpractice at the hands of a purely materialistic science. Their "abnormalities," treated as pathological, soon become so, and thereafter they may be committed to sanitaria or to insane asylums with every show of reason, and their psychism, which they can neither help nor successfully control, becomes the very cross on which they are crucified.

Not that it could ever become the crown of their salvation. Psychism is a dubious gift at best, a thing from which everyone might well pray to be delivered, but to deal with it as though it were a disease, makes it one. Rather it should be dealt with as though it were the smoke from some spiritual fire, for in most cases that is more nearly what it really is. And because fire smokes most when it smolders, psychism can be transcended by an increased intensity of spiritual life. By "spiritual life" I do not mean any kind of religious devotionalism; I mean the life which becomes possible through a completely unified consciousness. Psychism is not a disease, but it is usually a sign of dualism of one sort or another, and its effective cure is not in medication, regimentation, psycho-analysis, "mental treatments," or anything of that sort, but complete liberty of thought, action, and emotional expression given and gained through love and understanding. This alone will restore a unity of being which has been lost.

The lack of this love and understanding on the part of spiritual and medical advisers, friends, husbands, and lovers of these Delphic women who have become prematurely aware of the four-dimensional world is destroying in the bud a future blossom, thus delaying human evolution and the fulfillment of the Biblical prophecy that the heel of the woman shall crush the head of the serpent. Because the *intuitive*, man or woman, and not the captain of armies or of industries, is now the hope of the future—the highest human type.

"We antagonize on," as Emerson says, and who can doubt that at the appointed hour there will be a revulsion from all this destruction and slaughter, that the masculine cycle will be succeeded by a feminine cycle in which peace will prevail, and love and compassion triumph over hate and revenge. Astrologically, this has been long predicted in the advent of the Aquarian Age, and signs of it are not lacking: the leaders of almost all of the so-called spiritual movements of the day have been women— Madame Blavatsky, Annie Besant, Alice Bailey, Mary Baker Eddy, to mention four at random.

But the impending evolutionary advance of which I speak, foreshadowed in the growing power and importance of women here in America, cannot take place until the "waters"—by which I mean the women of that world—are stilled. And this can only come about when men and women cease to devastate and destroy one another—and more often than not in the name of love. Only by coming to a new understanding of the meaning and purpose of love, and on that understanding establishing a new kind of relation, can that sex-warfare cease, and the participants attain to liberation from their own narrower selves and from the coercion of one another—thus releasing a creative force heretofore prostituted to ignoble uses.

For most people, love means bondage of one sort or another, and this is because they try to subordinate love to themselves, to warp it to serve their own purposes. But it is impossible to subordinate love to anything, and it mercilessly revenges itself upon those little mortals who would subordinate God to themselves and make Him serve them. Those who try to escape the grip of this superhuman emotion by trying to fit it to the uses of an every-day mode of life will find that their prudences, their cautions, and their cowardice so dampen and pettify their passion that they rot and smolder instead of bursting into purifying flame. The measure of one's power to love is the measure of one's power to live, and to diminish love is to impoverish life.

In harmoniously adjusted natures, in the grip of the life-force, the movement of love is as ordained and inevitable as that of the stars in their courses: beginning on the heights as a spiritual experience, it descends in a long curve of beauty to those "ultimate delights" which are to true lovers a sacred ritual of the spirit. As is well known, that sex-instinct which ushers in the love-life and the religious sense awaken together, and are strangely and intimately intermingled. Sometimes they are scarcely distinguishable, religious ecstasy and sheer eroticism intoxicating the consciousness at the same time and in a similar manner. This is a mystery the meaning of which evades us, but its importance cannot be gainsaid, for it negates all those current materialistic conceptions of love as solely a biological necessity. At such a theory of love it is not necessary even to glance. Its answer to the question of why nature has so overloaded the sexual batteries—that the continuance of the race must be assured at any cost—is one of those half-truths, inducing error, the product of a materialistic habit of thought. Love insures the conservation of the species, yes, but also its lyrical expansion, for love has another function: to crack, and then disrupt the hard shell of the personality, permitting the release of the spiritual nature. All personal loves arising from a sense of *otherness*, however intense and exalted, are initial, and initiative of that love which is the sense of *oneness*, not only with the beloved, but with all the world besides. But that oneness can be attained only through that otherness: the path to the eternal is through the transitory.

"Only love and yet love, for in love is salvation," wrote my wife Eugenie's Oracle when she asked for instruction in these matters, and it had these revealing words to say about the problem which puzzled us, and perhaps has puzzled all true lovers:

The flow of sex withholds from growth so long as it is the passion of the blood. When it rises to the passion of the spirit it liberates, and that liberation is the ultimate result. The long struggle for mastery of the passion of the blood opens at last the door through which the spirit enters. It is strange that the one cannot come to birth without the long trial that plunges the soul through agonies of remorse.

The future of the human race, its degradation or its regeneration, may depend upon the determination of a relatively few individuals to serve love, to sacrifice themselves upon the altar of Eros, and, submitting to an inner control and direction, to follow, "not afraid with any amazement," wherever it may lead. The blasting and blighting power of love, when made subservient to the personal self, is well known, but its regenerative and creative power when received into the soul as a deity to be adored, remains to be revealed. When lovers realize that their deep desire for one another is the desire of a sundered god for self-realization through reunion with its divine counterpart, when they petition, in all humbleness, "What wilt thou have us to do?" who knows but what they may be vouchsafed some answer, wonderful and new?

Herein lies the most momentous and pressing of all human problems: how to love in order to receive the fullness of love's benison. Is it insoluble? Having wrested from life so many secrets, is this one to elude man to the end? Of one thing at least we may be certain: the answer must be sought not in the niggardly mind, but in the opulent heart.

This brings me back to my immediate subject, the true function of woman in the modern world. Not to remain a domestic drudge, to play bridge, to sell goods, or to hold office has her hard-won freedom been achieved. She has two major responsibilities: in her social life she must work for the establishment of a world-polity not founded on force, fear, or hate; in her personal life she must endeavor to enlarge and enrich the relation between the sexes, discovering knowledges, communions, felicities, unknown to that relation as it now exists. Of course man must coöperate in this emprise, but woman must assume the role of initiator and guide. Where but in the secret heart of woman is the right solution to be found? For her body is the temple of love's ritual, and the treasury of the continued race. A woman's mission now, not as a person, but as an incarnation of the Eternal Feminine, is to help man to redeem and make rhythmical his passional nature by bringing it under the domination of his spiritual will. Only by so doing can she achieve the deliverance of both from the evil effects of his disordered sexuality, his masculine heritage from centuries of sexual excess and irresponsibility resultant from the subjugation of woman. What interferes with woman's performance of this service is the very thing which has made it necessary: her slave psychology, her instinctive disposition toward acquiescence and submission, which is *her* heritage from that selfsame past—a woman's last word being, "I will speak thy speech, Love, think thy thought."

And so, through ignorance and inertia, man and woman, who should help one another to freedom and wholeness, torment, devastate, and corrupt one another, and "despoil the unborn." It has often been said that woman's love is in the last analysis maternal: that she yields soul and body to the beloved in the same spirit in which she gives her breast to a child; that her love is possessive and protective in the same sense and for the same reason. This is to a certain extent true, and it is beautiful; but in the new relation between the sexes woman must become more than mother if man is to become more than child—she will never win him from his wolfishness if she be content always to play the lamb-like part. In order that man and woman may have this new and true relation and function, both must transcend their naturalistic rôle and function, not by abrogation, but by sublimation, recognizing that, though they are children of earth, there are other realms to which they are also native. Thus may they enter into their divine inheritance. This they can achieve best with the aid of one another, through the transforming power of love alone—love, the miracle worker, which will teach them by what communions, contacts, caresses, by what synchroniety of vibration for the interchange of opposite polarities they will be able to bring about that consummation of each becoming the other and of both becoming the All. For the aim and end of love is freedom, but freedom of a strange sort, and arrived at in strange ways. Confounding and paradoxical is the arithmetic of the spirit! Two become one, but in becoming one, each becomes two—both build into themselves a reciprocal self with the aid of one another: through interdependence they win independence—the Divine Androgyne comes into being: the beyond-man is born.

Love is the ultimate desperate encounter: by means of it the life-force puts the personality on the pleasure-pain grindstone in order to bring it to a finer edge, make it a better tool with which to cut a nearer image of the superhuman archetype. Success dwells not in conquest, surrender, easy indulgence, or harsh denial, but in obedience to life's rhythm, submission to the determination and control of the life-force, whether it unites or parts, prompts to the giving of all to love or the leaving of all for love— whether it precipitates lovers into one another's arms, or between them lays a sword. It will do sometimes one and sometimes the other, according to which makes them a finer organ of its activity, or according to the particular "station of the cross" at which the eternal pilgrim is, on what is known as "the Path," that highway milestone by incarnations instead of by years.

XV

THE ANDROGYNE

ART IS RELATED TO LIFE MUCH AS MATHEMATICS TO discovery: that is, as a direction-finder and fore-shadower of things to come. There is truth in Oscar Wilde's famous paradox: "The function of life is to imitate art," because art represents the transcending of nature through the operation of a higher power of consciousness. Nature is the virgin gold and art the minted coin stamped with an image beyond the power of Nature to imprint—the image, namely, of the archetype. The sculptured gods of Hellas and the painted Christs, Madonnas, and Adams and Eves of the Renaissance represent, really, archetypal man and archetypal woman. By the contemplation of such images life is enlarged and ennobled, and this is what Wilde's aphorism implies.

But there is another and a different ideal of beauty than that of the manly man and the womanly woman which from far back has exercised a strange fascination on artists the world over, particularly in the Orient. This is the *divine androgyne*, or double-souled god. Represented sometimes as male, sometimes as female, it nevertheless partakes of the nature of both, the sex-indices not stressed, but represented merely by symbols, or else concealed altogether, as though by reason of a perfect inner polarity sex itself had been transcended, so that, complete and perfect, the androgyne had no polar counterpart of itself.

No base or vulgar suggestion inheres in that ambiguous and enigmatic beauty which Greek sculptors gave to their statues of Hermaphroditus, young Bacchus, Ganymede. It is a beauty rooted in the same idea which inspired countless representations of those world-saviors, Buddha, Christ, Maitreya; which lurks behind the smile of Leonardo's youthful John, Saint Anne's downcast lids, and which shines forth from the ruined lineaments of the Christ of the cenacolo—the idea namely that archetypal man is bipolar, and that the beauty in which masculine and feminine characteristics are mingled and blended is the most perfect beauty.

Every human being of either gender is potentially double-sexed, the sex of a person being determined by the predominance of the feminine over the masculine in the case of a woman, and of the masculine over the feminine in the case of a man. Sometimes, to be sure, the container—the body—fails to correspond with the contained, and this results in reversed and intermediate types, but these are rare.

This latent bisexuality is confirmed, rather than contradicted, by science, for it has been found possible to effect a change of sex in certain birds and animals by modifying the metabolism by means of diet. Science, however, advances facing backward, and in explanation of these mysteries gives only the dusty answer: "These are vestiges of a long-vanished past." But time is a womb as well as a tomb: the embryo exists that it may become a child; the child in order that it may become a man or a woman; and a man or a woman, did they but know it, exists to become man-woman. *Become what thou art! Be ye therefore perfect!* That perfection is nothing other than the divine androgyne.

The human correlative of the divine androgyne—its distorted shadow upon three-dimensional space—may sometimes be encountered in our great centers of civilization, for it is a type which gravitates to cities, though not necessarily of urban growth. It is something quite other than the physically double-sexed hermaphrodite—a freak of nature; it is not the man-soul in a feminine body or its reverse; neither has it any real relation to those unfortunate beings of either sex who have, through bad karma, early perversion, or sheer ennui, fallen into the pit of homosexuality. It is none of these, but a type quite definitely male or female in face, form, and function, though combining the qualities and attributes of both man and woman, often in such perfection and of so high a type that it would seem an effort on the part of nature to transcend itself—not to produce an abnormality, but to establish a new norm.

These *Uranians*, though they differ widely from one another, being essentially individualistic—"old souls," a reincarnationist would call them—possess qualities in common. They are proud, shy, sensitive, secretive—though this is often an imposed characteristic. They are highly intelligent, but even more intuitive, and not infrequently psychic—oriented, that is, in the fourth dimension, and responsive to those supersubtle currents of thought and feeling which pass independently of time and space as we have always conceived these things. They are powerfully imaginative, and this makes them creative, whether they are artists or not. They are also deeply spiritual, whether religionists or not. Possessing what is called a multiple personality, their most remarkable peculiarity is a certain *fluidity* —a protean power of subtle transformation, under the dominance of this or that mood during which their whole aspect changes, so that different people think of them differently, seeing the particular "self" which they themselves bring out. When the intellect and will are active, this self takes on a masculine aspect, even if the body be that of a woman; and when the mood is passive, compassionate, tender, there is an augmentation of the feminine, so that even though the person be male, the woman in him looks for the time being out of the windows of his eyes.

Balzac draws the portrait of the androgyne in its supreme manifestation in the character of Seraphitus-Seraphita, a mysterious being which to an enamored man seemed woman, and to an enamored woman, man. From some inner necessity, by reason of some chemical or alchemical power, that being manifested to each of them the qualities of the sex opposite, its complement and counterpart. *Seraphita* is perhaps the greatest and most profound mystical novel ever written. Balzac, with his gusto for corroborative detail, and his lust for thoroughness, plunged deep into the ocean of theosophical lore preliminary to his attacking of the subject. Except as to its setting—the icy north—and those other things which give the tale artistic verisimilitude, it was no invention of his own which he rendered, but a conception of superman held as a closely guarded secret from the most ancient times by the custodians of the Ancient Wisdom in the world.

The idea of the androgyne is not foreign to the thought even of materialistic science, as said before; but the loftiest religious philosophy is alone great enough to deal with this concept in any illuminating way, and it has always been an inexpugnable part of that philosophy, though concealed in symbols and referred to only in veiled terms. The swastika, the crux ansata, the hexagram, or "shield of David," the Rosicrucian rose and cross, and many other symbols variously represent duality in unity—the union of masculine and feminine in a single significant form. Swedenborg (from whom Balzac got his idea) taught that "eternal" man was androgynous—a union of the two sexes; so also did Blake, and many another mystic. Such too is the esoteric teaching of every great religion, and sacred scriptures, read in the light of this idea, take on new meanings. There is perhaps more than appears in such sayings as: "For in the resurrection they neither marry or are given in marriage, but are as the angels of God in Heaven," and in this enigmatic passage in the Apocrypha: "For the Lord Himself, having been asked when His kingdom should come, said: 'When the two shall be one, and the outside as the inside, and the male with the female!' "

The key to all such mystic symbols and cryptic sayings is contained in the fundamental concept of the Hindu-Aryan cosmogony with regard to creation. Brahma fell asunder into man and wife, and from the striving of these two sundered poles toward reunion "worlds were put forth." Each segment of the sundered god seeks its complementary self, and all life is an effort toward the restoration of an equilibrium disturbed by such action—a return to primordial unity, or pure being.

In the natural world this striving manifests as polarity; in human nature, as love. And just as all natural phenomena are in their last analysis electromagnetic, so also is love, the desire of the self for the Self, the motive force in human affairs. Upon this point the Upanishads are explicit: the (limited) self is the only lover and the (unlimited) Self the only beloved. Now all loving is becoming, and since the Self is both lover and beloved, the Self can alone become, and it can become only itself in the sense of self-realization—the realization that it is not limited, but free; not twain, but one. Self-realization, not as a person, but as a cosmic being, is the first cause and final effect of that long traffic between the sexes, of every kind and degree, on various planes of being, resumed life after life.

This is the reason why the love between the sexes is the supreme coercive force in human life: it is the supreme *transforming* force. The love of man for woman and of woman for man is the universal and ordained approach to that consummation variously called the finding of Christ, and the marriage of the soul with God. This marriage can take place only in the temple of a bi-polar or perfected body. Christ said: "Be ye therefore perfect," and love is the way to that perfection, because "he who loveth not, knoweth not God, for God is love." The saint and the mystic are not the only candidates for initiation through love; they only represent the later stages of an awareness attained by much loving in many lives. The quality and the direction of their love may appear far other than that of the generality of mankind, but it is the same ecstatic, transforming, regenerative emotion directed inward and Godward —instead of wasting itself in the vain pursuit of "self in others still preferred." In the long search for the Immortal Beloved through and by means of the love of persons, there comes at last the realization that the particular loved one is really only a window through which that Immortal Beloved is glimpsed, and from that moment the sun itself, the Golden Person, becomes the center of interest rather than the pane which it irradiates and through which it shines. Love is this worship of the divine through the human. Hawthorne had deep discernment when he wrote: /"God grant to each of them His love, and one human heart as its interpreter."

The total misconception of the nature of love—which is really everyone's love affair with the god within—together with our false and furtive attitude toward sex, produces mysterious maladies, psychic and physical, not to be medicined by any method which science knows. There is no longer any incentive to that mystical quest, that disciplining of the entire nature for the sake of love and by means of love whereby men and women might transform themselves more and more nearly to the archetypal pattern, the Divine Androgyne.

Now those *Uranians* who foreshadow, however faintly and imperfectly, this beyond-man type, are the ones best qualified to undertake this mystical quest, but they stand today in particular peril, for by reason of their sensitivity they are peculiarly susceptible to those psychic poisons with which the aura of every great city is charged—emanations of fear, hate, lust, greed, deadly depression. On their highly organized and impressionable natures these things operate in a manner and to an extent incomprehensible to the material-minded, to whom the unseen is the non-existent, the very coarseness of their fiber making them non-conductors, as it were.

Denied the sympathy and understanding of those about them, these unfortunate beings, in whom new potencies are stirring into life, the nature of which they are the last to understand, seek surcease from their ills by withdrawing from life through fear, or else by revolting against their environment. Because they have achieved that metamorphosis which makes them "different" through much loving in many lives, the need to give and receive affection is an imperious necessity of their nature; so they seek love, and because they are of so high a human type, they inspire love in others of a necessarily inferior type. Thus solicited, by nature generous and kind, their natural amativeness becomes a trap in which they either lie and rot, or extract themselves with much emotional rending, only again to fall a victim, self-beglamoured by their habit of idealization, their tireless quest of perfection.

Wounded in spirit, they may rotate away from every kind of amorous experience, but this involves

a kind of spiritual starvation they are the least qualified to endure. Some, therefore, find refuge in a relation with some kindred spirit of their own sex—
persuading themselves that they prefer moonlight
to sunlight—and some embrace an impersonal life of
service, achieving a purely negative happiness; still
others seek refuge in drugs, in drink, in promiscuous
and meaningless sexual relationships, or in suicide,
that quicker method of self-destruction, tragically
unaware that the Self, whose nature is eternalness,
cannot be destroyed.

In brief, these divinely ordained Discoverers, instead of adventuring boldly upon the vast, un-
charted oceans waiting to be explored, are driven
by adverse winds and currents to shipwreck on the
shoals of sensuality and sentimentality—their efforts
to free themselves only fixing them deeper in the
sand—or they dash themselves against the sterile
rocks of denial, and are broken by the very waves
by which they should be upborne.

In order to alleviate an existing condition it is
sometimes necessary only to call attention to it, and
such is my purpose here. Of succor for these endan-
gered mariners I have none, saving this presentation
of themselves, and the statement of their predicament.

XVI

MODERN IDOLATRIES

MAN IS AN INCORRIGIBLE IDOL WORSHIPPER. EVERY age has its particular idols, but there come sometimes crucial moments in the lives of nations when under pressure of suffering some spirit of newness, rising to the surface of life, destroys Bastilles, makes bonfires of Vanities, and overthrows those idols which men have erected as an outlet for their more impersonal passions, a justification for their excesses, and a focusing-point for their fears unconfessed.

Signs are not lacking that such a time is now rapidly approaching; that it may be, indeed, already here. But an idol is like a self-element, it must be known in order to be done away with, and it is therefore well to call attention to some of them. Nor need one be surprised at the names I give them, for an idolatry is always some good thing gone sour: an effort toward something better which through misuse or abuse has turned into something worse. It will still seem sweet to those to whom it was once sweet, and so the elder generation imposes it upon the younger, sacrificing youth upon idolatrous altars and making a merit of it.

Success is one of these altars. I have handled the bones of Carthaginian children taken from the ruins of the temple of Moloch, but I know parents who by pressure, precept, and example are even now offering up their own children on the altar of Success. I have witnessed the struggles of some of these sacrificial victims in the fierce fire of competition, lured there under pressure of that same *public opinion* which in Carthage made it a merit to serve the granite maw of Moloch with the flower of the youth of the land.

For there is something in the evil spirit of the times which dictates that everyone shall demonstrate, as early and as emphatically as possible, his *quality* not in terms of character but of accomplishment, whether commercial, professional, or scholastic: to make a lot of money, to write a best seller, to hold an exhibition, to win a prize or what not—to stick in one's thumb and pull out a plum and shout, "What a great boy am I!"

We are all of us open at all times to the power of suggestion—the gigantic fabric of modern advertising has been woven upon the discovery and utilization of that fact—but young people are particularly susceptible because they are unformed and uninformed, confiding, credulous. Therefore, all this success-idolatry, with its monstrous machinery of success-literature, success-lectures, success-advertising acts upon the plastic mind of youth in a manner little short of coercive: only the strongest and most independent can escape the infection of the success-first virus, administered as it is under the guise of business procedure, economics, practical psychology, and other resounding titles. There would be nothing wrong in all this if the ideal of success held up for emulation were the right one, but it is always the success which can be measured in terms of money, fame, social prestige, or power over others—the idea being that you haven't hit the bull's-eye unless you've made the bell ring: achieved *front-pageism*, in other words. If one of these success-experts were asked how to achieve unity of being, or that order of happiness and contentment which, according to Emerson is "the end of culture and success enough," he would be utterly at a loss, because his technique consists so largely in the arousing of fear—the driving of people success-ward through fear that they will not succeed—and fear is of course automatically destructive of unity of being, happiness, or contentment of mind.

And it is *fear*—always the dark shadow of idolatrous worship—which is corroding the secret hearts of so many young people today, inducing melancholia, a sense of inferiority, afflicting them with obscure nervous disorders, and sometimes even driving them to self-destruction. This subjective fear is kept alive and operative by the deliberate *appeal to fear* in success-advertising which, more literally than figuratively, hits them in the eyes wherever they look: the gigantic question mark, the pointed gun, the accusing finger, and all those warnings against every kind of infection which are themselves infections because they plant in the mind some new fear to be added to a long catalogue of fears. Moreover, the fear of failure which is the fertile cause of failure is fostered in schools and colleges through the mediumship of interscholastic elections, examinations, and all manner of quite unnecessary competitive tests, which, though designed to weed out the unfit, result more often in the humiliation and discouragement of the scholastic and social non-conformists— the very ones who, if differently dealt with, are likely to be found to contain the most precious of all human paste.

We, who are revolted at the very idea of child marriages in India, remain complaisant in the presence of these young, crushed lives, forced unions, and the wasting of the seed of talents still unripe.

We would make a bond salesman of young Hamlet, and encourage Ophelia to learn typewriting and stenography solely in order to become the secretary of that malefactor of great wealth, King Claudius. But bad as this get-rich-or-get-famous attitude is in the business and professional field, in the fine arts it is worse, because it incites to such a welter of inane and irresponsible production as to blunt those organs of receptivity and to impair that power of discrimination on which primarily a sound æsthetic depends—for the very word means *to perceive*. Furthermore, the compromises incident to the achievement of a swift success or to the making of a talent marketable are devastating to the artist: his Pegasus becomes a hack, art becomes an industry; for when the joy goes out of creation, the creative faculty soon ceases to function properly.

The animating spirit whereby a thing gets itself done determines its true quality and importance. This is the reason why the moment an artist begins to think overmuch about gain, fame, or praise, he ceases to be in the true sense an artist. For art is not a shop or a show-window where everything is displayed, priced, and advertised: rather is it a stadium for the development and exercise of latent greatnesses—the important thing in the practice of any

212

The Artist in Industry: Norman Bel Geddes' General Motors' Building at the New York World's Fair. Exterior and interior views.

art being not what the practitioner is able to produce, but what *it* is able to produce *in him*: what
effect it may have upon his consciousness. The true
artist spends his life wrestling with an angel without
hope of victory and with only the strengthening of
his spiritual sinews for reward. Great works of art
are only the by-products of this struggle—the spilt
blood of the conflict. A symphony by Beethoven or
a statue by Michelangelo is but the testament of
beauty-tormented spirits—bloodstains of love-battles
with their bright-dark dæmons who would give them
no rest.

To the young man or young woman, dimly aware
that the cruel every-day is capable of being trans-
formed into a festival of labor, love, and achievement, I would say: resist all efforts to make you bow
down to the Moloch of Success, for something glor-
ious and radiant awaits you if only you will *be true*.
Earn an honest living somehow, fulfill your obliga-
tions and clean up your messes—render unto Cæsar
—but everything beyond that which you are able to
wrest from life is your own, to do what you please
with; and do with it whatever pleases *you*. Devote
yourself to *the thing that thrills you*, for that is the
sure index of the direction in which your talents lie:
never mind whether or not it is profitable so long as

it is profitable to your happiness. This is the effective way of becoming a truly useful member of society because you will thus augment, by your own happiness, the sum-total of happiness in the world. You will, moreover, be by way of becoming a real human being instead of a standardized factory product, with however high a polish or however resounding a trade-name.

The second modern idolatry to which I would call attention is the exaltation and worship of the purely rational mind. Although the power to reason and form concepts has undoubtedly brought man to his present estate, and has given him his control over natural forces, that same analyzing, rationalizing, critical faculty—exalted above every other, and energizing in that waste land created by its own arid and devastating skepticism—bids fair to become the devil of the modern world.

Goethe was deeply right when he made his Mephistopheles the embodiment of the mental principle unconditioned by love or compassion and dedicated to the service of the will-to-power. Shakespeare was no less truly inspired when he showed his archvillain Iago to have the same psychological make-up. "Evil, be thou my good!" exclaims Iago, for to the mind "all things are equal"—the mind has a thousand "I's."

At the time of the Inquisition, religious idolatry waged war upon its protestants and challengers by means of the stake and rack. Men of the character and caliber of Galileo and Bruno, representatives of that skeptical, searching, scientific spirit all but universal today, were the sacrificial victims of that idolatry, and at the same time the emancipators from it. But now the worship of the rational mind has itself become an idolatry with a priestcraft of its own, scarcely less sinister in its compulsory power. From this idolatry we can only be delivered by the bold denial of the kingship of the mind.

I once spoke to the editor of a great Sunday newspaper of the gratuitous and irreparable injury often inflicted upon quite innocent persons by reason of his paper's policy of sensational and pitiless publicity. "The truth of the matter is," he made answer, "that a newspaper has no heart." And this is the truth also about our competitive, mind-worshipping, scientific-industrial civilization—it has no heart. It takes small account of man as a loving, suffering, dreaming, blindly-groping exile from the world of the wondrous, seared by tumultuous and irrational passions and strange desires, and transfigured by sacrifices and

215

self-immolations stranger still. In place of this willful-emotional man—which everyone secretly knows himself to be—we are asked to believe in such phantasms as the "economic man," motivated only by his material needs and moving only in the two directions of production and consumption; or in the "rational man," proceeding always from premise to conclusion, and acting always according to the dictates of his reason. Into such two-dimensional molds the priests and inquisitors of our mind-worshipping, mechanistic civilization seek to press multi-dimensional man, but signs are not lacking that, spiritually awakened, he will break those molds, and discredit that priestcraft as surely as when, mentally awakened, he broke the mold made by superstitious monkish monasticism.

For it appears to be a law of human evolution that we must throw down the very ladders up which we have just climbed; so that now, in order to attain the next eminence, we must reject the rationalistic ladder in order to erect the intuitional one whereby we may mount to an apprehension of the fourth-dimensional aspect of the world. Ouspensky names this "the fourth form of the manifestation of consciousness": it may be described as synthetic reason, just as the reasoning faculty, which is its third form, yielding the sense of three-dimensional space, is synthetic perception—perception being in turn synthetic sensation.

These revolutions, which like those of a wheel seem necessary for progress, are difficult and disturbing: the necessity for discovering in the god of yesterday the devil of today, and in the god of today the devil of tomorrow. But man's only adversary is, and can only be, what he has been, just as his only "comforter" is that which he must become.

The present is called the age of reason, because we have enthroned the rational mind, and strive to shape our lives in all things according to its dictates. But into the sanctuary now penetrates a voice which says: *The mind is the slayer of the real: let the disciple slay the slayer.* This sounds as blasphemous to the ears of mind-idolaters as *I will believe only what my senses report and what my mind approves* must have sounded to the dogma-idolaters of an antecedent cycle. But the sovereignty of the rational mind has at last reached its term, and for the following reason:

With the ascendancy of the rational mind, power over evolution passes from the group-soul (or from *Nature) to the individual. Further evolution can result only from the conscious effort toward growth on the part of the individual. Man, not striving toward evolution, not conscious of its possibility, not helping it, will not evolve. And the individual who is not evolving does not remain stationary but goes down, degenerates: that is, some of his elements begin their own evolution, inimical to the whole.

Now when this happens the mind itself is one of those elements which evolve in a manner inimical to the whole. That is to say, for those individuals in whom the growth of love and compassion has not kept pace with their mind-development, devolution will set in—they will become dualistic, pluralistic. This is exactly what is happening today to great numbers of persons of the advanced mental type: they have lost their unity of being, and the only way in which it can be recaptured is by a consciously undertaken polar reversal by reason of which, for the time being at least, the *woman* in them is exalted above the *man*. They must *slay the slayer*—the mind must be made subservient to the whole.

The third modern idolatry I have in mind is the most deeply vital because it has to do with sex.

The amorous embrace, the sexual orgasm, when uninduced and unaccompanied by supersensuous emotion, are not different from "a shot in the arm"

or alcoholic stimulation. But to the completely unified consciousness dominated by love, they are the
translation in terms of physical sensation of the ecstasy of such domination: they are symbols of it,
because they stand for and serve to represent it in
the same sense that a strain of music stands for an
emotion or that a sentence stands for a thought.
Such symbolizations are *agents of realization* by the
personal consciousness of something super-personal,
in the same way that the golden image or the ivory
crucifix are agents of realization of the peace of
Buddha or the sacrificial suffering of Christ. But
when love is merely and purely personal, when it is
regarded as a possession, instead of as an agent of
realization of the life-force, the sexual ritual degenerates into a mere indulgence, loses its efficacy, and
there are only feathers where there should be wings.

Now this is exactly what has happened: instead of
discovering in sexual love an agent of regeneration—
the sacramental bread and wine—we have become
idolaters: love has been slain upon the sexual altar
by our materialization of a mystery. This is the fertile cause of those excesses, perversions, and mor-
bidities with their aftermath of emotional misery and
physical disorganization which make sex a guarded
wound. The healing of this wound is not by sex-

education of the current sort—though this may have its uses—nor by prohibitions and regimentation supposedly conducive to "morality." The remedy must come rather from that order of sex-sublimation and self-discipline which inevitably accompanies the realization that sex derives its every value from *the magnitude of its coefficient*. This is nothing other than the quality and degree of *love* involved in any relation, and the conscious and intensive cultivation of that *true* love which alone is strong enough to overcome lust because the life-force is then in control. The victims of lust are those who do not love *truly* nor *enough*. Lust awakens only "the toad within the stone," but the desire of the true lover for the truly beloved awakens pity, affection, awe, aspiration, and —given appropriate circumstances—every noble and generous emotion possible to man. And who knows to what greater heights the worship of Eros is capable of carrying us? Blake says, "The whole creation will be consumed and appear infinite and holy, whereas it now appears finite and corrupt. This will come to pass by an improvement of sensual enjoyment."

XVII

EMERSON: MOUTHPIECE OF THE
AMERICAN SPIRIT

"AMONG SECULAR BOOKS, PLATO ONLY IS ENTITLED TO
Omar's fanatical compliment when he said, 'Burn
the libraries, for their value is in this book.'" So
wrote Ralph Waldo Emerson; but lo! he himself
turns out to be the Plato of the golden age of American letters, so that at this crisis of our national life
one is tempted to declare of his writings what Omar
did of the Koran, because through him, more powerfully and more perfectly than any other, the American Spirit speaks. That voice, if heeded, might conceivably precipitate action of liberation as it has
done before, for it is said that Lincoln wrote his
Emancipation Proclamation under the stimulus of a
lecture on human bondage he heard Emerson give.

Be that as it may, Emerson belongs to the great
hierarchy of prophets and sibyls, and the "sibylline leaves" on which his prophetic utterances
were first recorded are the leaves of those journals in which he jotted down his thoughts as
they came, and from which he later extracted his
various essays and addresses. Like the first rough

sketches of an artist, these journals are more charged
with the man's essential spirit than are his more considered, arranged, and prepared writings. In the
former, however, the nuggets of pure Emersonian
gold are so embedded in masses of memoranda, observation, quotation, and commentary, as to turn
away all but the most ardent, so that for the most
part this is a terrain explored only by the most tireless prospectors. Of these I count myself one, and I
have the pleasure here to present a few specimens
quarried from a re-perusal of Journals XLI to XLV,
embracing the years 1849 to 1854, chosen for the
most part with an eye to their present use and value.
They have lost none of their luster, either of thought
or expression, being curiously contemporaneous on
both counts. This is because Emerson was himself
one of those men, whom he describes, "who hits by
the health of his sensibility the right key, and so
speaks that everybody around him or after him, aim-
ing to talk of and to the times, is forced to quote
him, or falls inevitably into his manner and phrase."

In nothing is Emerson more of today than in a
kind of skeptical humor indulged in almost alone
in the Journals—a humor conscientiously excluded
from his more serious works. He had his pet aver-
sions, and one of these was the towering historian

of that day. "What a notable green-grocer was spoiled
to make Macaulay." "No person ever knew so much
that was so little to the purpose." Emerson recog-
nized a stuffed shirt when he saw one, however
highly placed:

Hurrying America makes out of little vanities its
great men, as, now, the three leading men in America
are of a small sort, who never saw a grander arch than
their own eyebrow; never saw the sky of a principle
which made them modest and contemners of themselves. Yet Washington, Adams, Quincy, Franklin, I
would willingly adorn my hall with, and I will have
daguerres of Alcott, Channing, Thoreau.

Liberty was the burning political issue then, as it
is now, but with the difference that it was only the
right of liberty to the slave which was in question.
Yet as a comment upon certain aspects of the American scene, how contemporaneous is the following:

The vulgar, comprising ranks on ranks of fine gentle-
men, college presidents and professors, and great Democratic statesmen bellowing for Liberty, will of course
go for safe degrees of liberty—that is, will side with
property against the Spirit, subtle and absolute, which
keeps no terms.

223

Liberty is indeed the recurrent theme of this volume of the Journals, because it was written at a time when Emerson was most profoundly stirred by the iniquity of the Fugitive Slave Law, and the capitulation of New England to the southern planters through its representatives, Curtis, Webster, and Choate, "statesmen and political leaders, always men of seared consciences, 'half villains,' who, it has been said, are more dangerous than whole ones." Emerson thus felt and expressed the humiliation of it: "There is a curious shame in our faces. The age is convict, confessing, sits on anxious benches." But more often, even when the outlook was darkest, he reaffirmed his belief in the ultimate triumph of the Abolitionists, thus formulating what he named "the austere law of liberty":

That it must be reconquered day by day, that it subsists in a state of war, that it is always slipping away from those who boast of it, to those who fight for it.

He cherished no animosity toward evil men because of his deep understanding of the nature of evil, and its essential impersonality. In the following he is not speaking of "half-villains," but of "pestilent rats and tigers," of which there would appear to be more eminent examples in our day than in his:

The existence of evil and malignant men does not depend upon themselves or on men; it indicates the virulence that still remains uncured in the universe, uncured and corrupting, and hurling out these pestilent rats and tigers, and men rat-like and wolk-like. Synesius said, "The calamities of nations are the banquets of evil dæmons." They hurl out, now a soldier, now a jesuit, and now an editor, a glozing democrat, as an instrument of the evil which they inflict on mankind.

Emerson's analysis of the English character, made in 1854, is truly clairvoyant—prophetic also, for what he said might happen to England in a time of stress, such as the present, *is* happening: the elimination of its "fops and bankers" and the release of what he calls its "war-class."

England does not wish revolution or to befriend radicals. Therefore, you say, England must fall, because it is moderate; mixed aristocratico-liberal or finality politics will put it in antagonism with the republicanism when that comes in. Yes, but England has many moods, a war-class as well as nobles and merchants. It began with poverty and piracy and trade, and has always those elements latent, as well as gold coaches and heraldry.

It has only to let its fops and bankers succumb for a time, and its sailors, ploughmen, and bullies fall to the front. It will prove a stout buccaneer again, and weather the storm. . . . England can only fall by suicide. English, the best of actual nations, and so you see the poor best you have got.

Commenting upon the solidarity of England, more manifest now and in the first World War than in his day, Emerson says:

I think the English have a certain solidarity; not an unaccountable sprinkling of great men here in the midst of a population of dunces, not a talent for this or that thing, as an idiot is skilful sometimes in bees or herbs, but what they have learned they record and incorporate, and have multitudes sufficiently taught to keep and use it. What Newton knew is now possessed by the corps of astronomers at Greenwich and Slough and Edinburgh and Glasgow.

Because of the all-inclusiveness of his vision, Emerson is the great master of generalization and discoverer of archetypes. This constitutes him, by his own standard, an aristocrat of aristocrats, for he says: "I call those persons who can make a general remark, provided also they have an equal spirit, aristocrats. All the rest, in palaces or in lanes, are snobs, to use the vulgar phrase." Here follows a fine example of the profundity of his insight and the greatness of his sweep. If to the catalogue of *isms* contained therein, Fascism, Socialism, and Communism were added, it could easily appear an admonition to us of today:

History of ecclesiastical councils arraying nations for and against some clause or quibble in a creed, and sucking the blood and treasure of ages to the one or the other part, as in the controversies of Europe on the Nicene and Athanasian, or of the two sects of Mahomet,—or of Catholic and Protestant later, or now of Mesmerism, etc., are all only valuable after ages have cleared away the smoke with the lives, cities, and institutions of the parties, and disclose the structure of mind which necessitates these heats and rages.

And the temptation is too great not to quote this one also for its appositeness:

It would seem all legislatures are alike, for Pepys says, his cousin Roger P., member of Parliament, "tells me that he thanks God, he never knew what it was to be tempted to be a knave in his life, till he did come into the House of Commons, where there is nothing done but by passion and faction and private interest."

Women's Rights had not become an issue in Emerson's day; there were, however, premonitory stirrings, particularly in New England, of which Concord, where he lived, was the spiritual center, for in the following excerpt from the Journal he declares his own convictions on this subject in no uncertain terms:

Woman. I think it impossible to separate their education and interest. The policy of defending their property is good; and if the women demand votes, offices, and political equality, as an Elder and Eldress are of equal power in the Shaker Families, refuse it not. 'Tis very cheap wit that finds it so funny. Certainly all my points would be sooner carried in the state if women voted. And the new movement is only a tide shared by the spirits of man and woman, and you may proceed in a faith that, whatever the woman's heart is prompted to desire, the man's mind is simultaneously prompted to execute.

Here follow his reflections on what must have been one of the first political assemblies of women, held in Worcester, October fourteenth, 1851:

Today is holden at Worcester the "Woman's Convention." I think that as long as they have not equal rights of property and right of voting they are not on the right footing. But this wrong grew out of the savage and military period, when, because a woman could not defend herself, it was necessary that she should be assigned to some man who was paid for guarding her. Now, in more tranquil and decorous times it is plain that she should have her property, and, when she marries, the parties should, as regards property, go into partnership full or limited, but explicit and recorded.

For the rest, I do not think a woman's convention, called in the spirit of this at Worcester, can much avail. It is an attempt to manufacture public opinion, and of course repels all persons who love the simple and direct method. I find the evil real and great. If I go from Hanover Street to Atkinson Street,—as I did yesterday,—what hundreds of extremely ordinary, paltry, hopeless women I see, whose plight, inscribed on their forms, "Leave all hope behind," is piteous to think of. If it were possible to repair the rottenness of human nature, to provide a rejuvenescence, all were well, and no specific reform, no legislation would be needed. For as soon as you have a sound and beautiful woman, a figure in the style of the antique Juno, Diana, Pallas, Venus, and the Graces, all falls into place, and men are magnetized, heaven opens, and no lawyer need be called to prepare a clause, for woman moulds the lawgiver. I should therefore advise that Woman's Convention should be holden in the Sculpture Gallery, that this high remedy might be suggested.

This final quotation from the Journal has so vital a bearing upon our national predicament at this particular moment of time that one can only again say of Emerson what he himself said of Plato: "We run very fast, but here is this horrible Plato, at the end of the course, still abreast of us. Our novelties we can find all in his book. He has anticipated our latest neology."

Has any voice sounded so true and high a note as this? Is it not indeed the timeless voice of the American Spirit which here speaks? Attend and consider well the following:

Heaven takes care to show us that war is part of our education, as much as milk, or love, and is not to be escaped. We affect to put it all back in history, as the Trojan War, the Wars of the Roses, the Revolutionary War. Not so; it is your war. Has that been declared? Has that been fought out? And where did the Victory perch? The wars of other people and of history growl at a distance, but your war comes near, looks into your eyes, in politics, in professional pursuit, in choices in the street, in daily habit, in all the questions of the times, in the keeping or surrendering the control of your day, and your horse, and your opinion; in the terrors of the night; in the frauds and skepticism of the day.

The American independence! That is a legend: your Independence! That is the question of all the present. Have you fought out that? And settled it once and again, and once for all in the minds of all persons with whom you have to do, that you and your sense of right and fit and fair are an invincible, indestructible some-what, which is not to be bought or cajoled or fright-ened away. That done, and victory inscribed on your eyes and brow and voice, the other American freedom begins instantly to have some meaning and support.

XVIII

PREPAREDNESS FOR PEACE

I READ THE OTHER DAY THAT AN INTERNATIONAL committee had been organized to formulate basic principles for a future society in a new world-order. This is a hopeful sign of the times, whether it results in anything or not, for it represents a longer view and a deeper sense of responsibility than those ordinarily held at this time. However prolonged the present World War may be, it must come to an end, and that end may come quickly, dramatically, unexpectedly. In either case it will find us unprepared for peace. From the preparedness for war in which this country is now engaged—the organization of death—it will not be easy to switch quickly to preparedness for peace—the organization of life. Preparedness for war is what precipitated the first World War, which only prepared for this one. Long before that first World War happened, my friend Harry Barnhart saw in a Belgian railway station soldiers of four different European countries, each in a different uniform, each with a clanking sword attached to his waist, and in a moment of clear vision he knew then and there that the countries they represented

232

would one day be fighting one another, as indeed they did. The consciousness contains the event which shall befall. It is in this way that nations and individuals create their own destinies.

H. G. Wells declared in a recent broadcast that after this war mankind must turn wholeheartedly to the search for truth. He seemed to think that science had all the answers, but has it? Science has destroyed many illusions, but on the other hand it regards as illusions many things which may be as true as what we call scientific fact. By reason of increasing pressure from the archetypal world, the world of causes, the ever-thinning veil between the physical and the astral worlds will be broken down. This is only another way of saying that consciousness will be sensitized to higher vibrations, and one of the results of this will be that the materialist will be discredited in the face of overwhelming evidence that there is no death. That evidence, indeed, exists already, for those who seek it, but that is just one of those things which the orthodox scientist goes out of his way not to seek.

New forces now operating in the protosphere of the planet and in the human consciousness make miracles, which are simply phenomena counter to the current thought of the time, not only possible, but inevitable. Does this surprise you? It has been predicted for two thousand years, and of late reasserted and reiterated by what I have named "the Delphic Sisterhood." Scant heed has been paid to these prophecies, however, on account of the deep distrust of the rationalistic thinker for the intuitive perceiver. I am, as you know, a believer in the Delphic gift, and I desire here to record certain prophetic utterances. Let me quote first from Nancy Fullwood, the Introduction to whose book, *The Song of Sano Tarot*, I wrote, and whose psychism I described in my autobiography, *More Lives Than One*. She speaks here not in her own person, but as the mouthpiece of a higher intelligence, as did the oracles of old:

It is impossible for me to explain to you in human terms just what will take place in your living and in the life of the planet now that the darkness has been dispelled and the light of the spirit has found an outlet. Rapidly it will permeate the earth, and I assure you that there will not be an atom which will not find new life and increased energy . . . Do not be startled with any phenomenon that might present itself to you. You will soon realize that what you have called psychic phenomena will now be the order of the day. New ideas will enter the consciousness and new creation will make a new world, and the old dark and uncertain world will exist only as a dream. A new and vital force is permeating the earth. Every living thing will be renewed.

It is better by far to look up and out in full consciousness of this new power. To those who walk in confusion and darkness I would say that their confusion and darkness will be intensified by the light. So it is the part of wisdom to become aware of the light. Never cease striving even though you are surrounded by darkness through which no light penetrates. I assure you that the day will dawn when you yourselves will have pierced through that veil, and will bathe in the light behind it. Do not hold to discords in your own lives or in the lives of others. Remember always that where harmony is not, no good can be. Dispel all selfishness and greed, for they are poisons in the sacred blood of man. It is such a simple matter to turn your attention to others rather than to center it on yourself. When you let go of self you will feel an actual soaring of your spirit into light and beauty. It is truly profoundly magical, and there are no mortal words to describe its power.

The atmospheric conditions about the earth are changing rapidly, and it is difficult for some people to move with the new movement of life. The best method of moving with the new vibration is stillness. That may seem strange, but man never moves so swiftly as he does when he is still. You all know this truth, but it cannot be repeated too often at this time. Bear in mind what I have said about stillness.

Here is food for thought, and incentive to action —but of a kind which may seem like inaction, being "action of liberation," achieved in stillness. This is Yoga: "In sitting still he travels far." It is Tao: "The sage does nothing, and everything is accomplished."

The Western consciousness is too exclusively centrifugal. This results in a great deal of meaningless activity and shallowness. We need the corrective of the contemplative life: the life of inner activity in order to repair the ravages of too much running about. It is just as necessary to a healthy and harmonious existence as is the physical need of sleep. There are times when our interest in the external world should cease; when we should draw up our bridges, so to say, interrupt all external communication as far as possible, become isolated in our own fortress, and seek the strength which silence gives.

I was taught these things by teachers in whom I had confidence; I tested them out, and found that they "worked" when put into practice. Always a prospector for that truth which is beauty, because I have been assiduous in this quest, I have been helped in strange ways. There was a musical comedy of a few years back called *I Married an Angel*. That describes what I feel about my own second marriage, for my wife, Eugenie, was an alien here, but at home in some other world which I learned to regard both as more real and more sublime, even though I could not enter it except through her. She was endowed with faculties and powers of which orthodox science does not admit the existence; and was in communication with a seemingly supernatural intelligence—though perhaps only her own higher consciousness—and to this entity she gave the name of "Oracle." The manner of communication with it was by automatic writing. Of these sibylline leaves I preserved a great number, and edited and published them after her death, a living testament of her transcendence. Here are a few quotations which seem to me to have a bearing upon the subject of this lecture:

We told you that a new growth of faith was coming. The voice of us will ring so clear that the blindness of the intellect cannot stifle the call we make . . . In the future men are to be more aware of us: the spirit of us will so joyfully shake them that they will cry out. "Rejoice, for the Light that so long has been lost to us through the darkness in which we have been wrapped, is to be broken by the Light that shineth always to illumine the hearts of men." . . . All men will rise and join in a mighty chorus of praise to the power that today they seem not to realize. Truly men are being chosen, gathered into groups, and from these groups shall go forth brotherhood filled with action of liberation as none have ever been . . . The future lies with the men who realize the spirit as the potent force by which alone the physical may be completely conquered. The next century will open a period of occult development in which the race will rapidly develop a great new sense . . . The days to come will see greater changes in the current of life than has been known by the race now living, and a new principle must come into life, if the opening of new horizons is to bring knowledge, and not cast into chains men of the new race . . . The way of strife leadeth to the final battle, after which the forces of brotherliness will bring harmony into the lives of the followers of Us . . . The days that follow are full of possibilities to make concrete our Being in the hearts of men. The future is to the Light-bearers.

I have become a champion and defender of Delphic women in a world where I find them persecuted and derided. In consequence of this I have been blessed by them and helped by them. This help and blessing I want to pass along to others by giving these prophetic utterances for inspiration, for guidance, for incentive to a new kind of action in this dark hour.

These lectures represent my best possession—the stored-up honey garnered from a long and various experience in many different fields. When the house is on fire, one throws everything one wishes to save out of the windows in the hope that even at the worst some passing stranger may be benefited by what would otherwise vanish in flame and smoke. Well, the house *is* on fire; Madrid, Barcelona, Warsaw, Antwerp, Berlin, London, Leningrad, and other cities have been attacked by fire from the skies. This fire is but the symbol of that more subtle fire referred to in these and other oracular messages, wherewith the soul of humanity will be seared, purified, and at long last redeemed. Of all my possessions, I regard these oracular messages as the most precious, because they emanate from some dimension of consciousness to which I myself have not been able to attain. I have saved them therefore until the last, and I toss them now to the beloved reader in the hope of achieving for these lectures some such catharsis as was achieved in *Hamlet*, with the line:

And flights of angels sing thee to thy rest.